RELAXATION

NTC Publishing Group

TEACH YOURSELF BOOKS

RELAXATION

James Hewitt

NTC *NTC Publishing Group*

Long-renowned as *the* authoritative source for self-guided learning – with more than 30 million copies sold worldwide – the *Teach Yourself* series includes over 200 titles in the fields of languages, crafts, hobbies, sports, and other leisure activities.

This edition was first published in 1994 by NTC Publishing Group, 4255 West Touhy Avenue, Lincolnwood (Chicago), Illinois 60646 – 1975 U.S.A. Originally published by Hodder and Stoughton Ltd.

Library of Congress Catalog Card Number: 93–85118

Printed and bound in Great Britain by Cox & Wyman Ltd., Reading, Berkshire.

Contents

sleeping. Letting go for sleep. Sleeping position. Other
methods. On awakening.

Introduction

Why learn to relax? The most direct and simple answer, and a powerful one, is that you will feel so much better once you can relax well. Relaxation is not a panacea for all major modern ills, but it does go a considerable way in alleviating many personal problems, particularly those related to anxiety and stress. And its benefits are more far-reaching than is commonly understood.

You may proceed with learning to relax in full confidence that the results can only be beneficial – to health, to bodily and mental efficiency, and to the quality of your emotional and perhaps even your spiritual life. There is no illusion, no trick of autosuggestion. The enhanced sense of well-being is not 'all in the mind'; it has a sound physiological basis.

The total human organism benefits from the practice of deep relaxation: you start feeling calmer, happier, more harmoniously in touch with life. Studies conducted in medical laboratories have recorded the physiological bases of such feelings: reduced heart rate and oxygen consumption, neuroendocrine integration, more symmetrical brain wave patterns, and so on.

Probably the most common reason for a man or woman reading a book or joining a class on relaxation is to meet a personal need for reducing so-called nervous tension. Millions of westerners suffer from the harmful effects of tension.

Though some tensions are a normal and necessary part of living, without which motivation to take action might be curtailed excessively, there is wisdom and practicality in aiming to eliminate *unnecessary* tensions or at least to reduce them to manageable intensity. Tension often disrupts physical efficiency and clear thinking, whereas attention to the messages conveyed by normal tensions leads to appropriate action being taken.

In this book you will find a step-by-step guide to teaching yourself to relax deeply. Instruction will also be given in how to make the best use of your acquired relaxation skills in the course of day-to-day living.

Two main methods of eliciting the relaxation response are described. Both methods are practical and within the capabilities of almost everyone. Both should be learned. Thereafter you can decide for yourself whether one or the other should predominate in daily practice or whether they may be given equal weight.

One approach is through neuromuscular relaxation – becoming aware of tension in the voluntary muscles of the limbs, trunk and face, and then eliminating it. By relaxing these muscles you not only experience physical rest of great depth and quality, but also calm the nervous system and mind.

The second main approach is through the mind itself. Several million westerners now know the value of meditating in the eastern way; most of them are practising meditation primarily for the body–mind relaxation and the stress-release it affords. In this book we will be concerned with what might be described as the bare technique, which laboratory studies have shown to elicit the deep rest and the benefits of the relaxation response. The techniques may be practised without any doctrinal tie-ups, and there is nothing mystical or exotic about them. Meditation for relaxation requires only quiet sitting and breathing, simple psychological devices and the right attitude to them.

Dipping deeply into the relaxation experience, you develop a natural tendency to carry physical and mental relaxation into day-to-day activities. I shall show you how to make relaxation an inseparable and valuable part of your life.

Posture and body use are of great importance in relaxed and poised living, and detailed instruction is given in Chapter 4. There are also chapters on using relaxation to improve the quality of your sleep, and on relaxation therapy. There is a chapter on coping with harmful emotions, and another on coping with anxiety and nervousness when facing situations you find important, such as competitive and public performances. Relaxation and poise improve your chances of doing well at such times.

Finally, some pointers will be given to the kinds of attitudes which relaxation practice promotes. By that time you should have begun to understand that the art of relaxed and poised living may be taken to rich and even profound levels.

1

Arousal and Relaxation Responses

On the threshold of the twentieth century, a distinguished Hungarian scientist, Dr Francis Volgyesi, made a cogent prediction: 'Unless we alter our way of living,' he warned, 'the next century will be in the first place the age of "nerves".'

The nature of twentieth-century civilisation has indeed been such that descriptions similar to Volgyesi's have become familiar. Our times have been variously dubbed, with similar implication, 'the aspirin age', 'the age of anxiety' and, most recently, 'the age of stress'.

What is stress?

Firm definitions of stress are few, considering the many books, medical papers, magazine and newspaper articles that have been written about it. Those definitions there are differ in two main respects, according to whether emphasis is put on the *stimuli* responsible for adaptive wear and tear or on the *reaction* to the stimuli or wear and tear itself.

Dr Herbert Benson, in *The Relaxation Response*, makes the former emphasis, defining stress as 'situations leading to continuous behavioural adjustment'.

Most scientific definitions, however, highlight the *response* and the *experience*. A helpful, standard definition is that given by Dr Richard Mackarness in his book *Not All in the Mind*. 'Stress', he wrote, 'in scientific terms, is the wear and tear induced in the body by the adaptive day-to-day struggle of the organism to remain normal in the face of potentially harmful agents, including physical and psychological stressors of all kinds, from bad food to noisy neighbours.'

The popular, public view of stress equates it with emotional distress, whereas the scientific view encompasses both physical and psychological stressors of all kinds – not only anger and fear, frustration and anxiety, but also cold and heat, polluted air, physical injury, and so on.

The popular view of stress can, with advantage, be kept in the forefront of our minds, for psychological distress is the major factor in suffering adaptive wear and tear in modern life, and it produces the kind of stress for which relaxation is well equipped to deal.

There is another difference between the popular and the scientific views of stress: the scientist includes in his definition events and emotions that are normally considered to be desirable and pleasant experiences. Welcome events, such as a marriage or the arrival of a baby in the family, may have an element of strain in them. The sudden good news that a person has won a fortune on the football pools or in a sweepstake may engender enough excitement to bring on a heart attack; less obviously stressful may be some other life changes, such as falling in love or having a holiday.

The Cluster Theory
The inclusion of welcomed events among stress factors is surprising, if at all, only on first impression. A little thought will show that there are few events that evoke unmixed emotions, and that some stress accompanies most predominantly happy events, such as getting married, celebrating Christmas, or gaining promotion in a job or profession.

That the general public is aware of this is shown by a scale of stressful events drawn up by Drs Thomas H. Holmes and Richard H. Rahe, psychiatrists at the University of Washington Medical School. They gave a list of forty-three commonly occurring events in human life to 394 men and women of varying ages and social backgrounds and asked them to rate the events mathematically for their stress impact, with the most stressful rating 100 'life-change units and the others graded down the scale. As a fixed point to work from, they were told that a marriage was assessed at 50 units. The basis of judgment was the effort of adjusting required in living through an event. Drs Holmes and Rahe called their list 'the social readjustment rating scale'. When ratings averages were calculated, the death of a spouse was ranked at the maximum 100 life-change units.

The psychiatrists' follow-up experiment was to see if there was a correlation between the amount of adjustment coming close together in a person's life and the chances of contracting an illness.

In their follow-up studies, Drs Holmes and Rahe found that ten times more widows and widowers died during the twelve months following the death of a husband or wife than all other people in their age groups. They also found that illness was twelve times more likely during the year following a divorce than for married persons during a corresponding year. A further discovery was that when several life-change events on the inventory come together or cluster in a twelve-month period, susceptibility to illness is raised significantly. The highest susceptibility to illness comes during the months *following* the period of stress rather than during it.

High life-change-unit scores in a period of twelve months were found to increase significantly the chances of falling ill. A score of less than 150 units gives a thirty-seven per cent probability of becoming ill within the next twenty-four months. A score between 150 and 300 units raises the illness probability to fifty-one per cent. A stress impact rating of over 300 life-change units is highly dangerous, for research shows that there is then an eighty per cent chance of illness occurring within the following two years.

Alarm at these figures may be tempered by three considerations. First, the figures in the social readjustment scale are averages of the assessments of 394 persons. The figures have been found to be statistically valid for the prediction of raised illness probability, as stated above, but the impact of life-change events varies considerably according to individual temperaments and conditioning, and the event's circumstances.

A second point to note is that research subsequent to the first studies by Holmes and Rahe shows that when changes are *welcomed* the stress impact is greatly reduced. When life-changes are not welcomed, their adjustment impact is maximised according to the strength of feeling one has about them.

The third influencing factor is the cultivation of relaxation and stress-reducing techniques. Relaxation skills and attitudes defuse the impact of life-change events.

8   Relaxation

Social Readjustment Rating Scale

Life event	Life-change units
Death of spouse	100
Divorce	73
Marital separation	65
Jail term	63
Death of close family member	63
Personal injury or illness	53
Marriage	50
Fired at work	47
Marital reconciliation	45
Retirement	45
Change in health of family member	44
Pregnancy	40
Sex difficulties	39
Gain of new family member	39
Business readjustment	39
Change in financial state	38
Death of close friend	37
Change to different line of work	36
Change in number of arguments with spouse	35
High mortgage	31
Foreclosure of mortgage or loan	30
Change in responsibilities at work	29
Son or daughter leaving home	29
Trouble with in-laws	29
Outstanding personal achievement	28
Wife begins or stops work	26
Begin or end school	26
Change in living conditions	25
Revision of personal habits	24
Trouble with boss	23
Change in work hours or conditions	20
Change in residence	20
Change in schools	20
Change in recreation	19
Change in church activities	19
Change in social activities	18
Moderate mortgage	17
Change in sleeping habits	16
Change in number of family get-togethers	15
Change in eating habits	15
Holiday	13
Christmas	12
Minor violations of the law	11

Stress factors in modern society

If we touch briefly on some of the stressful features of modern society, it should be in the understanding that it is a one-sided picture that is being presented. But by looking momentarily at the problem we can see better what needs to be done to realise the contrasting image – that of enjoying an age full of challenge and interest in the fullness of poised living.

The human organism has to make continual adjustments in the environmental field, which normally it is well equipped to do. The maintenance of homeostasis (internal, physiological equilibrium) is an ongoing process that ends only with the death of the individual. But today, life in advanced countries poses special problems of adaptation to ever more rapid change – and for many people the wear and tear is showing. Wear and tear, as we have seen, is one definition of stress.

Material and technological development in the twentieth century has been marked by concomitant increases in the strains and stresses under which individuals live. One hundred years ago, in America, Thoreau remarked that people lived lives of 'quiet desperation': if he were alive today he would surely express himself more strongly.

Occupational strain

'Executive stress' is one of the cliché terms of our times, linked with an image of a harassed businessman wincing at a stab of pain from a stomach ulcer. But technological complexity, the pace of modern life and the prevailing competitive spirit mean that *many* jobs can be stressful. (Equally research studies show that being unemployed may be even more stressful than having a responsible job. A significant increase in illness and premature deaths is linked with increasing unemployment.)

Studies conducted in Europe and in the USA show the influence of occupation on the incidence among workers of high blood pressure, coronary heart disease, duodenal ulcers and diabetes. These diseases were most prevalent among workers whose jobs entailed high levels of responsibility.

A study by Sidney Cobb and Robert Rose of American air traffic controllers working for prolonged periods of high alertness found a much higher frequency of hypertension, duodenal ulcers and diabetes in the controllers than in those actually flying the planes.

Piloting a passenger aircraft is itself one of the most stressful occupations, which is why periodic tests are made of a pilot's blood pressure, heart rate, and so on. His emotional health is just as important as his physical fitness – and it can deteriorate in a few minutes. In America, Holland, and some other countries, following an air crash, an autopsy on the body of a pilot is extended to a 'psychological autopsy'. Often it is found that the pilot had emotional problems at the time of the crash. A few hours after a pilot has passed a medical examination, he may be unfit to fly because he has had a row with his wife.

The problem for men and women in jobs involving high responsibility and peak alertness is to successfully 'unwind' after a day's work. This is aided immeasurably by acquiring skill in body–mind relaxation.

Stress diseases
Some distinguished physicians have been warning that psychosomatic disorders and stress diseases have increased alarmingly. Most prevalent of the dangerous diseases associated with stress are high blood pressure (hypertension) and coronary heart problems. High blood pressure is sometimes described as the 'hidden epidemic' – because it develops slowly, and there are few, if any, symptoms. Then suddenly there may come a heart attack or a stroke.

Several factors are believed to be responsible for the prevalence of hypertension and heart disease in developed countries. High levels of saturated animal fats in the diet is a much discussed factor, and insufficient exercise another. Stress, too, is linked with hypertension.

There is statistical evidence linking stressful living with high blood pressure. More black than white people suffer from this disease in the United States, but the distinction applies only to blacks living in the urban ghettos. Black people living in rural areas are not particularly prone to hypertension, and those who live in the middle-class suburbs of cities have a rate only half that of black people living in crowded inner city areas in conditions where we would expect to find considerable emotional stress: anxiety, hostility, violence, frustration, and insecurity.

One would expect to find above average incidence of high blood pressure in people with responsible occupations. Studies show that this is so, as we saw in the study of air traffic controllers. City bus drivers suffer more hypertension than their colleagues who collect the fares. Exercise levels may be a contributing factor, but a study made of Dutch postal workers showed that the *responsibility* of the job was a more significant factor in raising blood pressure than the amount of exercise a worker had.

Dr Herbert Benson, of the Harvard Medical School, says: 'Doctors have recognised for years that stress is taking a toll. It is not difficult to understand the correlation between the highly competitive, time-pressurised society in which we live and mental stress with its influence on heart disease.'

A stressful emotion, such as anger, can cause a build-up of fatty substances – such as cholesterol and triglycerides – in the blood, which may stick to and harden on the walls of the arteries, narrowing them.

In one study, when the blood of racing car drivers was tested, triglyceride levels were high just before and during a race and remained at twice the normal level three hours after the race had ended. On the other hand, serum cholesterol levels are raised as a result of *prolonged* stress. Tax accountants who were studied showed raised serum cholesterol levels in the month of April, the tax deadline period, and the levels fell during May and early June.

During an alarm or stress response cortisone levels in the blood go up, and high cortisone levels have been known to damage heart tissue.

Two American physicians, Meyer Friedman and Ray H. Rosenman, have studied the personality traits and life styles of thousands of people with heart disease to see if any factors were present that could be distinguished from the personalities and life style of people with healthy hearts.

As a result of their investigation, Drs Friedman and Rosenman were able to describe two contrasting personality types: one prone to coronary disease and one with a high chance of avoiding it. The first, the Type A personality, is ambitious, aggressive, impatient, self-demanding, and nearly always in a hurry. The second, Type B personality, is less rushed off his feet or out of his mind (it's usually 'he' rather than 'she'), less ambitious, has a better (more philosophical) perspective on things, can enjoy the present moment, is rarely impatient, and does not make excessive demands on himself.

In short, the Type A personality suffers nearly continuous psychological stress, while the Type B personality corresponds to the relaxed person living a poised life. This book could be described as a guide to how not to be the overstressed 'type' (Type A) and to become the relaxed 'type' (Type B). The Friedman/Rosenman study suggests that thereby we will be helping our hearts.

Some studies suggest that stress weakens the body's defences against infectious diseases, that the capacity of the immunity system to destroy invading bacteria is impaired when there is an excess of stress-response steroids in the blood.

The link between executive stress and peptic ulcer is public knowledge. 'This job is enough to give me an ulcer,' we hear the decision-maker say. And very often it does. Indigestion at times of emotional tension is a commonplace occurrence. Emotional arousal stimulates the production of digestive acids in the stomach: if the stomach is kept empty, these acids may literally burn a hole in the lining of the duodenum.

Some investigators have attempted to link mental stress with cancer; the claim is controversial, but there have been some interesting experiments in this area of enquiry.

A Soviet medical scientist painted the skin of rats with a carcinogenic substance. The highest incidence of resulting skin cancer was in those rats that were subjected to stressors producing anxiety. Rats kept in a tranquil environment had few instances of skin cancer.

Animal experiments show that when animals are stressed repeatedly their immunity system breaks down. The stress can be psychological as well as physical. If harmful emotions like anger and fear cause a breakdown in our defences, does it follow that integrating feelings and attitudes such as hope, faith and courage will strengthen them? Some physicians and doctors are saying that attitudes of mind can be responsible for a breakdown in health or impairing healing, and also for preventing illness or recovering from it.

Harmful emotions

In the course of social history an important change has developed in the nature of the predominant stressors that people have to cope with. The main stressors that people face in modern society are not physical assaults – wounding by an enemy, the bite of a wild animal, or extremes of heat or cold – but something subtly and insidiously dangerous, undermining health slowly and stealthily. Most human stress is now caused by psychological stressors. These emotions mostly do not flare momentarily: they take possession of the body and their effects may last a long time.

The mind, through feelings and emotions, can make a heaven or a hell of living experience. It can also produce physiological changes that are conducive to developing a disease.

Damage to health may be caused by anger, rage, frustration, hatred, envy, jealousy, and resentment; also by fear, anxiety, worry, and guilt. Pleasant emotions and feelings may sometimes be stressful when they cause excessive or prolonged excitement, but we should concentrate on the main danger, which comes from the distressing emotions and feelings named above.

Nearly all emotions are mixtures of several feelings; sometimes what seem to be opposite emotions, such as hatred and love, may be experienced together. But if you look closely at the range of distressing emotions, you will see that they are variations of two primary emotions: *anger* and *fear*.

Anger is linked with the impulse to attack or fight and fear with the impulse to escape or flee. This is the basis of the *fight or flight response*, the alarm reaction to danger, which we have inherited from our primitive hunting ancestors.

Anger is the most immediately dangerous of emotions. It is fired by the frustrations of modern living, and more often than not has to be denied expression.

Raw anger and raw fear are less often met in life today than their more subtle and sophisticated variations – hostility and anxiety. Anxiety has an element of fear in it, but unlike fear, which has a clear object, anxiety gathers around anticipation of something not formulated clearly but perceived as threatening to body and/or the ego's security. Anxiety may also be due to unconscious fear, so that the person experiences an anxiety state without being able to say why. Though without a clear object, the anxiety is stressful.

Some psychologists take the view that anger and fear go together: not anger and fear, but *anger-fear*. We fear to some extent that which makes us angry, and are angry at that which makes us fearful or at ourselves for being afraid. A 'cornered' animal or person, unable to flee, fights back.

'In psychopathology', A. H. Maslow and Bela Mittelmann wrote in *Principles of Abnormal Psychology*, 'it is better to speak of a single entity, fear-anger or anxiety-hostility. . . . The simple fact of the matter is that, where the individual's self-esteem or feeling of security is threatened, he will feel *both* afraid and angry. Introspectively or unconsciously, both will be felt; sometimes one, sometimes the other, will predominate.' And then they say: 'The somatic pattern involved is *one*.'

Let me make this last point clear: *in both anger and fear the same basic state of body arousal occurs*. This is the *fight or flight response*. In anger the reaction is a tendency to fight, whereas in fear the tendency is towards flight.

The fight or flight response

Early in the twentieth century, Walter B. Cannon, an American physiologist, pioneered study of the alarm or stress mechanism, which he called the *fight or flight response*. Later other researchers, Dr Hans Selye in particular, built up a more detailed picture of the physiology of the alarm reaction and increased understanding of why and how prolonged stress causes physical illnesses.

The coordinated fight or flight response developed out of an animal's, and primitive man's, need to take action on the perception of threat, the action taking the form of either aggression or running away.

Those body organs ill-equipped to support fight or flight, such as the digestive system, are inhibited and those organs and processes able to further the action prepared for are activated. Salivation stops and the mouth feels dry. Blood pressure goes up. The heart beats faster. The breathing rate and oxygen consumption increase. Less blood goes to the organs whose function has been inhibited, more blood goes to the brain and to the skeletal muscles, to aid quick thinking and quick action respectively. An electroencephalograph (EEG) reading shows increased electrical activity in the brain, and other machines show muscular tension as the muscles stay alert for action. The liver secretes more sugar to fuel muscle activity. The adrenals excrete adrenalin. Among the parts of the brain activated is the motor area which causes muscles to contract ready for movement. If no movement follows, the muscles may stay tense for some time. The pupils of the eyes dilate, for better seeing, and the sense of hearing becomes sharper. The body has mobilised automatically to become a more powerful and effective fighting or fleeing machine.

'The key to these marvellous transformations in the body,' W. B. Cannon wrote in *The Wisdom of the Body*, 'is found in relating them to the natural accompaniments of fear and rage – running away in order to escape from danger, and attacking in order to be dominant. Whichever the action, a life-or-death struggle may ensue.'

Life-or-death struggles? Few of us know anything about them today. But we are all familiar with bouts of anxiety, anger, resentment, envy, and other emotions which also activate the organism – not so dramatically as in a life-or-death confrontation, but sustaining arousal for a long time. The body is mobilised for action that the circumstances of social life today do not allow to be taken. (A worker taking a dressing down from an employer has to grimace inwardly and bear it!). The result is overtaxing of body organs and a possible breakdown of health. A primitive arousal state is too crude for dealing with problems of human relationships in a complex society.

Fighting and hunting man knew when and why his alarm bells were ringing, why he had to attack or run. And he *did* fight or flee, so that arousal chemicals only stayed in his blood for a short time. But modern man has to cope with frequent or long-term states of arousal. An imagined or anticipated injury or threat is responded to with the same stress reaction as to an actual injury or real danger.

The organism subjected to prolonged strain often succumbs to disease. What this disease will be depends on where the main weakness is located in the individual organism, which is influenced by external and internal conditioning, genetic make-up, age, sex, previous health history, and so on.

How stress damages health

How can anxiety or depression produce a physical illness? How can not having a job cause premature death?

A detailed account of the physiology of prolonged stress need not be given here; this can be found in books on this subject. I will mention just one important feature.

Classic experiments in this area were conducted by Dr Hans Selye, Director of the Institute of Experimental Medicine and Surgery at the University of Montreal. When rats Dr Selye had subjected to prolonged stress were dissected, they were found to have considerable enlargement of the adrenals, which had also a dark discoloration due to congestion and discharge of fatty-secretion granules, shrinkage of the thymus and the lymph nodes, and bloody stomach ulcers.

'The adrenalin was flowing,' thrill-seekers say, reflecting on an exciting experience deliberately chosen. Living for excitement is a kind of adrenalin addiction. The effect of tense excitement will be minimised if appropriate physical action is taken with it and the emergency chemicals in the blood have a chance to clear before the next bout of tension. But if the state of alarm persists for hours, days, weeks, or months, the adrenal glands and other organs are overworked like those of Dr Selye's rats.

Professor W. S. Bullough, of Birbeck College, London, and other researchers have shown that an excess of adrenalin in the blood slows down the repair of tissue and the renewal of cells. Tension keeps adrenalin at high levels in the blood, whereas the output of adrenalin is reduced during relaxation or sleep, promoting repair and renewal in the body. That is why relaxation supports the healing of skin cuts and wounds, and tension retards healing.

The relaxation response

Situations in life which pose a threat or require radical adjustment tend to evoke the fight or flight response, with its high physiological arousal: quickened heart rate, faster breathing, increased metabolism, and so on. There is, however, an opposite response that is less well-known, less often written about, than the alarm reaction. This contrasting response, which is also innate, is one of low arousal in which most body organs 'take it easy'. The body passes into a state of rest of extraordinary depth – deeper in some respects than that of deep sleep.

The 'discovery' of the *relaxation response*, though only in the sense of describing the physiology of something innate in human beings for thousands of years, must be credited to Dr Herbert Benson, Associate Professor of Medicine at The Harvard Medical School and Director of the Hypertension Section of Boston's Beth Israel Hospital.

Detailed scientific description of the physiology of both alarm and relaxation reactions had to await the development of medical technology to the point where changes in the body associated with these responses could be measured. Scientific investigation of the relaxation response did not come until the late 1960s and early 1970s – and it came about in an interesting way. Chance frequently takes a directing hand in important scientific advances, and it was so in this case.

In 1968, Dr Benson was working, with associates, at the Harvard Medical School, studying the relationship between a monkey's behaviour and its blood pressure. He was approached by several enthusiastic practitioners of transcendental meditation. They asked him if he would monitor their blood pressure during meditation, for they believed they were lowering it during meditation. At first their suggestion was turned down, but the meditators continued to request laboratory study until Benson agreed. His study of the physiological changes produced by a simple method of meditation continued for some years as he put together the pieces of what he saw as an innate human response of extraordinarily deep rest that could protect people from the harmful effects of stress reactions and act therapeutically. He described this very restful state, which he called the relaxation response, in medical papers and his book *The Relaxation Response*, published in the mid-1970s.

What main physiological changes are found in the relaxation response? And how do they compare with those of the alarm or the fight or flight response? The answer is that in most ways the changes in relaxation are in the opposite direction to those in arousal. The contrast is striking, and significant for any person seeking to enjoy protection against stress and other benefits of relaxation. Table 1.1 summarises the results found.

Table 1.1 The physiological changes of the Fight or Flight Response and the Relaxation Response compared

	Fight or flight response	*relaxation response*
Heart rate	increases	decreases
Blood pressure	increases	decreases from higher levels
Breathing rate	increases	decreases
Oxygen consumption (body metabolism)	increases	decreases
Blood lactate levels	increases	decreases
Sympathetic nervous system activity	increases	decreases
Parasympathetic nervous system activity	decreases	increases
Alpha waves	decreases	increases
Muscle tension	increases	decreases

The first thing to note in the physiological changes associated with deep relaxation is that the heart rate is lowered. Dr Benson and colleagues noted an average decrease of three beats per minute in the volunteer meditators studied. The work the heart has to do is lessened.

The breathing rate slows down, and breathing becomes quieter and more rhythmical.

The main physiological change Dr Benson discovered in the meditators, who meditated for twenty to thirty minutes following a similar period of just sitting quietly, was a marked decrease in oxygen consumption and metabolic rate. Body cells use oxygen, which is carried in the bloodstream, to burn food fuel. Metabolism is the process by which nutritive material is built up into living matter or broken down into simpler substances. Body metabolism decreases in the relaxation response, so that Dr Benson refers to it as a hypometabolic state, whereas the fight or flight response he calls a hypermetabolic state. During the relaxation response body energy requirements become very low. Metabolism decreases to a point only otherwise found in deep sleep or in hibernating animals; but the deep relaxation state differs from both sleep and hibernation.

The pattern of decreasing oxygen consumption in sleep is a gradual progressive fall, bottoming out after five to six hours. In the meditators studied oxygen consumption fell to a point below that of deep sleep during the first three minutes of meditation. And their brain wave rhythms were different from those of sleeping people.

In states of hibernation, rectal temperatures fall. This does not occur in persons eliciting the relaxation response. It seems that deep relaxation is a unique state, different from sleep or hibernation.

Another interesting change belonging to the relaxation response is a marked decrease in blood lactate, a substance that gets into the blood as a result of the metabolism of skeletal muscles. Blood lactate levels fell sharply during the first ten minutes of meditation at a rate more than three times faster than the normal fall in people sitting at rest.

It is interesting to find that high blood lactate levels are associated with states of anxiety. In an experiment carried out in 1967 at the Washington University School of Medicine, in St Louis, patients suffering from anxiety neuroses were injected with either a non-active salt solution or a solution of lactate. The effect of the salt solution was a reduction in the number of anxiety attacks, but nearly every patient given the lactate solution had more frequent anxiety attacks. When people in 'normal' health were given injections of lactate, twenty per cent of them experienced anxiety attacks.

The fall in lactate levels is consistent with decreased activity of the sympathetic nervous system, which is activated during the fight or flight response. Another branch of the involuntary nervous system, the parasympathetic, is associated with the calming of the body and with the relaxation response.

The control centres for both the arousal of the alarm response and the slowing down of the relaxation response are in the hypothalamus, at the base of the brain. Dr Walter R. Hess, a Swiss physiologist who won the Nobel Prize, produced the fight or flight response in a cat by electrically stimulating a part of the hypothalamus. But he found there was another area within the hypothalamus which when stimulated produced the opposite physiologic changes to those of the emergency reaction. He called it 'the trophotropic response' and said it is 'a protective mechanism against overstress belonging to the trophotropic system and promoting restorative processes.'

Dr Benson considers that his relaxation response and Dr Hess's trophotropic response are different names for the same deeply restful state of the human organism. 'The relaxation response' is an ideal term for the layman or laywoman to use, as it clearly depicts the decrease in activity in the body.

When electrical activity in the brain during the relaxation response is measured, slow rhythms called *alpha waves* appear almost immediately and increase in frequency and in intensity as the relaxation procedure continues. For most people, alpha wave patterns are associated with relaxation and a sense of well-being. The brain wave patterns recorded during sleep are different from those of deep relaxation.

Relaxation of the skeletal muscles is a very significant change for us to note, for these muscles come under conscious control and awareness. Relaxation of the skeletal muscles is therefore an important method of letting go from tension and eliciting the relaxation response. In this book, I advocate the practice of both progressive muscle relaxation and meditation.

Finally, what happens to a person's blood pressure during deep relaxation? It was the certain feeling that Dr Benson would find that blood pressure would be lowered during the practice of transcendental meditation that took the first volunteers to his laboratory. Dr Benson found that meditation brought down their heart rate, oxygen consumption, breathing rate, blood lactate levels, and muscle tension. But the volunteers' blood pressure was *not* lowered.

If Dr Benson, who had been researching the causes of hypertension, was dismayed by this finding, it was not for long. For he also found that these meditators, who were mostly young and healthy, had healthy low levels of blood pressure before, during, and after meditation. He immediately asked himself if there was not a relationship between their healthy blood pressure levels and the practice of meditation. If people had *high* blood pressure, would practising meditation bring it down? When this was put to experimental test, it was indeed found that meditation – or the experiencing of the relaxation response by another method – will decrease blood pressure from above normal levels. If the blood pressure is already normal, it will stay at that level.

So we see that we are not helpless victims of stress. It can be reduced to acceptable levels. We may even join those people who may be said to 'thrive on stress' – or, rather, what to many other people would be stressful. This means being active in problem solving, in taking responsibility, and welcoming change, complexity, and competition, with no diminution of a sense of well-being.

Herbert Benson believes that the integrated relaxation response is important to modern man. It is, he says, 'an innate mechanism within us', 'a universal human capacity', and 'a natural gift that anyone can turn on and use'.

How *can* we turn it on? Dr Benson's initial research showed that one form of eastern meditation could elicit the state of deep rest. Later investigation led him to write that other forms of meditation were also effective, as were several different relaxation methods used therapeutically in the West. With a little training, most people can enjoy the physiological and other benefits of the relaxation response virtually at will. And most people can learn to live more relaxed lives in general.

2

Relaxed Living:
The Antidote to Stress and Tension

Broadly, there are two distinct ways of reducing the amount of strain and tension suffered in life.

The first way is to avoid, eliminate, or modify the stimuli responsible for the problem. Some stress can be avoided entirely by making sure you are not placed in the situations that cause it. Other environmental changes may not remove a cause of stress, but make it more bearable and less damaging to health and peace of mind. This first approach has its limitations.

Complexity, competitiveness, and change have brought much stress into living. These components of modern society are likely to continue to grow and intensify, as they have been doing for more than a hundred years. While we can make minor adjustments to our home environment that make for more relaxation, there is little or nothing we can do about tackling the major stress-producing features in society at large. This is where the second way of reducing stress come in.

As the environment becomes more complex and 'difficult', whether we like it or not, what we should do is to teach ourselves to cope more effectively – which means changing fundamentally how we *react* to external and internal stimuli. Changing ourselves offers more scope for improvement than changing the environment, which is rarely ours to change. In the first chapter we saw the influence on the body and mind of two contrasting reactions – one of alarm and high arousal and the other of tranquillity and low arousal.

Before outlining the main components of an overall strategy for coping effectively with tension and stress, it is necessary to look momentarily at the most popular, yet unsatisfactory, ways of coping with stress.

Pills, alcohol and smoking

The three most popular ways of coping with tension in Western society are by taking a tranquillising pill or an alcoholic drink, or by smoking a cigarette. They are unsatisfactory 'solutions' in several ways. First, they are artificial aids and inferior to natural relaxation: both as methods and in the quality of the altered consciousness. They protect, when they do, by dulling or distorting the response to stimuli. They can become addictive and can damage health. Lastly, to continue to have a stress-blunting effect, they have to be used in progressively stronger measures.

Pills

Drugs have their medical uses when doctors have to deal with severe problems in their patients. But many doctors have voiced concern at the over-prescribing of drugs, in particular those aimed at reducing nervous tension and mental distress. Nearly half the drugs prescribed by British doctors are tranquillisers, anti-depressants, and sleeping pills. A report issued by the Royal College of General Practitioners said that the use of minor tranquillisers and hypnotics in Britain increased by twenty per cent between 1965 and 1970 to nearly fifty million prescriptions annually. The figures are higher today. In 1980 it was estimated that one in five British women and one in ten British men were taking mind-altering drugs. About one million of them were taking the tranquilliser Valium. Dr Peter Parish, author of the report, said:

> The increase in the prescribing of CNS [central nervous system] depressant drugs suggests that general practitioners are blanketing their patients' emotional reactions to an excessive degree and they must ask themselves whether it is right for them to produce a pharmacological leucotomy on contemporary society.

Americans swallow so many tranquillising and anti-depressant pills that in 1971 Senator Edward Kennedy asked the US Congress to write into the Congressional Record a paper warning about the dangers of 'internal pollution'.

For most doctors and most patients, the 'answer' to nervous tension and anxiety is a tranquillising drug. Some persons take them daily over a period of years; for great numbers of users, breaking the habit of taking tranquillisers leads to unpleasant withdrawal symptoms, which resemble those of acute anxiety attacks but belong to a true withdrawal syndrome. This difficulty may occur in persons who have only been taking the drugs for a few months and in small doses.

Another drawback of drug-induced relaxation is the 'blanketing' of sensory awareness and emotional aliveness. Tests show that reaction times may be slowed down and judgment clouded.

Alcohol

Alcoholic drinks may be enjoyed for the pleasure they give and as a proven social lubricant – but alcohol is an unsatisfactory solution to coping with tensions for similar reasons to those given above in connection with taking tranquillising drugs. There is the danger of physical dependence; the slowing down of reaction times; the impairment of intellectual sharpness; the clouding of judgment. There is, too, the temptation to drink too much and possibly enlarge and damage the liver. Alcohol slows down brain activity. There is a foetal alcohol syndrome: children born to alcohol-drinking mothers may have smaller brains and an 'oriental' appearance characteristic of the syndrome. Individual responses vary and researchers are uncovering some of the reasons why some people become physically dependent on alcohol and why some people are physically harmed by alcohol more readily than others.

On the brighter side, there is some evidence that persons taking one or two drinks a day have less cardiovascular disease than non-drinkers. The alcohol inhibits the action of platelets, minute bodies in blood, concerned in clotting; the blood stays less sticky and the blood vessels more open. The danger exists in relation to a diet high in saturated fats. Examination of blood samples shows that if wine is taken with a fatty meal, the platelets have got up to less mischief than if no alcohol had been taken with the meal.

Smoking

People smoke cigarettes to gain relief from nervous over-activity and tension. When an anxiety state is virtually chronic, smoking is often excessive and a danger to health in ways that have been well publicised. Tobacco is a stimulant, not a relaxant, activating increased production of the stress hormone noradrenalin; yet smokers at the first twitch of anxiety will reach for cigarette and lighter. Why do smokers find that smoking relieves anxiety? The answer must lie in part with 'the placebo effect', but there is also the consoling ritual of the physical act of smoking and the equally consoling sensation of sucking. The ritualistic factor is very marked in the lighting of pipes: think of Simenon's Inspector Maigret and certain non-fictional politicians. Desmond Morris, in his book *The Human Zoo*, calls smoking a displacement activity, busying the hands to take the attention away from worries and anxieties. It is also, some psychologists tell us, a form of 'oral gratification' – like sucking the thumb or a dummy-tit in infants.

Because the adrenals have been activated, smoking raises blood pressure and also the amount of cholesterol and other fatty substances in the blood. That smoking is linked with cancer of the lungs is well known, but it is not fully understood why only a minority of smokers are so affected. Less well known is that cigarette smoking contributes to as many deaths from cardiovascular disease as it does to those from lung cancer. Men who smoke more than twenty cigarettes per day are three times as likely to die of heart disease as non-smokers. Children born to smokers tend to be underweight.

Smoking distorts sensory awareness. Sensitivity in tasting foods is impaired, and strong-tasting foods may be sought to penetrate the 'screening' smoking has established.

Marihuana is smoked by many thousands of people, despite its illegality in many countries, again largely because it induces a more relaxed state, a temporary euphoria and flight from the world's and personal cares.

A connection between cigarette smoking and nervous tension is indicated by the fact that after taking up relaxation practice, smokers usually reduce the number of cigarettes they 'need' to smoke in a day, and many give up the habit entirely. Smoking is as much a symptom of nervous tension as a means of trying to reduce anxiety. Similarly, as people become more adept at relaxation skills they usually cut down on tranquillisers and sleeping pills, often to the point of being able to give them up entirely. The consumption of alcohol is also likely to be reduced, in cases where people have been drinking large amounts, because of the 'cushioning' effect.

When relaxation/meditation has been used as a therapy for drug addicts and alcoholics, significant successes have been obtained, despite the power of such addictions. Asked why they were able to much reduce or give up drugs or alcohol, the patients involved in these experiments spoke of the superior quality of relaxed consciousness to drugged consciousness or an alcoholic haze. In relaxation/meditation the 'I' is in control at all times and not under the influence of a chemical.

If one or more of your own ways of coping with stress has been mentioned in this section, ask yourself now: Why artificially induce states of relaxation by methods which may harm your health and which dull senses and mind, when self-directed relaxation releases tension more effectively and enhances the senses, mental faculties, and the quality of living experience in general?

It remains for me, in the remainder of this chapter, to encapsulate the natural, self-directed approach to coping with tension and anxiety, without recourse to drugs or artificial aids to relaxation.

The way to relaxed living

How should we go about attaining deep relaxation and relaxed living? The way to combat stress lies mainly in adding to the strengths we have to resist it and to the skills we can acquire to dodge or deflect its assaults or to neutralise their impact. The strategies and tactics we employ to realise these ends add up, collectively and in practical terms, to *relaxed living*.

We go straight for the most direct and practical, simple and effective techniques, with scientifically proven records of bringing about real relaxation, and requiring no equipment, either technological or what might be called conceptual or cultural, such as some specific religious belief. Our focus is on living *experience*. This is open to people of all belief systems, except perhaps those engendering a fanaticism incompatible with any worthwhile state of relaxation. The essential thing is to start practice and discover what the experience is like, giving it a fair trial over the coming weeks.

Earlier it was said that there are two broad approaches to influencing the amount of stress in our lives: one concentrating on the external, environmental forces responsible for stress and the other on how we *react* to events. Our main attention should be given to our reaction, but this does not preclude making any alterations to the environment or the external circumstances of living in as far as this is possible and beneficial.

You can change your immediate environment in ways that make life easier, ranging from introducing some things into your home to please eye and perhaps ear or reducing clutter to a greater semblance to order, to finding a new job or moving to a more restful neighbourhood. As training in relaxation progresses, most people experience a natural build up of motivation to make changes in environment and lifestyle in the direction of greater relaxation.

You can also keep a wary eye on the frequency of your more important life-change events, in the light of their stress ratings, as tabled on page 8. Avoid, when possible, clustering too many important changes in any period of up to twelve months. Most life changes are unavoidable, in any normal life. If you have a high score of life-change units over a period of several months, you should seek to minimise the danger to your health by giving extra time and attention to relaxing frequently, maintaining a balanced, nutritious diet, taking adequate exercise and your normal hours of sleep, avoiding situations likely to be stressful when possible, and otherwise taking good care of yourself.

When you cannot change the stimuli, you may be able to modify your reaction to the stimuli. In most situations in which a tensed person reacts in an alarmed, excited way, triggering the fight or flight response, a relaxed person is aroused either not at all or only mildly.

Relaxation is nature's antidote to stress, and scientific studies of the fight or flight response and its opposite relaxation response, recounted above, has shown us why.

The key question now is: what are the best ways to elicit the Relaxation Response?

In *The Relaxation Response*, Dr Herbert Benson lists several techniques, some from the East and some from the West, which he says produce physiologic changes associated with the relaxation response. In this book we concentrate on two of them, chosen for their simplicity, directness, and fundamental importance to relaxed living. I have also had to consider the suitability of relaxation methods for the general reader. The first method is relaxation of the skeletal muscles from scalp to toes, including the muscles of speech and visual imagery which are connected with our thinking. The second method is basic essential meditation, whose efficacy Dr Benson proved by scientific testing. *Both* methods should be learned, for reasons which will soon be explained. Both produce physiologic changes seen in the relaxation response. They can be practised singly or in combination. They have complementary influences in relaxed living. The first acts primarily through the body and the second through the mind, though each produces body–mind relaxation.

The ability to relax your skeletal muscles is the foundation of relaxed living, on which all else may be built. The main technique of muscle relaxation described in this book is a simplified and shortened version of progressive relaxation, which is a twentieth-century therapeutic method pioneered by Dr Edmund Jacobson in the United States.

Autogenic training and autohypnosis are two more practices on Dr Benson's list of those with the capacity to trigger the relaxation response: however, they have certain features which make their strictly formal practice not quite suitable for the general reader.

The body's skeletal muscle system gives us a practical point of entry into controlling the arousal mechanism. Muscle tension is a sign of an aroused state of the organism, but when electrical activity in the muscles is low, arousal everywhere in the body becomes low. Muscle relaxation and a calm state of body and mind go together, so that to attain the former is to realise our aim of relaxing body–mind.

Muscular relaxation is a neuromuscular skill, which is learned through daily practice. Learning is made possible by developing the kinaesthetic sense, the sense by which we are aware of tension or relaxation in our muscles. Another practical factor is that we have voluntary control of our skeletal muscles: you can decide to lift a cup of tea to your lips and drink, then do so. We will make use of this muscle control in learning to recognise tension and to let go from it.

The second approach we will make to eliciting deep psychophysical rest is through the mind. The practice of meditation (Chapter 7) uses simple psychological techniques whose results will delight most newcomers to such practice. For thereby consciousness is lightened of its burden of anxious thoughts and the body sheds its tensions and settles down to the deep rest of the relaxation response, as scientific investigation has showed. Dr Benson extracted the bare psychological bones of meditative practice, and has himself used meditation successfully with his patients. When meditation is used for the purpose of relaxing body–mind, it becomes practical, non-sectarian, and free from exoticism.

Just as the body feeling learned through the practice of muscle relaxation may be carried advantageously into everyday activity as *dynamic relaxation* (Chapter 4), so, too, the feeling of mental relaxation associated with meditative awareness may infuse day-to-day consciousness. This is one reason why I said that the practice of *both* methods is valuable and that each practice complements the other. Further, the ability to let go from tension in your muscles from scalp to toes enhances the practice of meditation by removing the distractions of muscle tensions and, in turn, the practice of meditation will aid the process of focussing attention on your muscles to relax them.

Though meditation has not been exclusively an Eastern concern, it has been widely accepted in the East for thousands of years and there we find the largest body of literature on its theory and practice. On the other hand, the stressful conditions of Western life in the twentieth century led to the development of detailed instruction in muscle relaxation as part of therapy for stress illnesses. So in your relaxation practice, following the instructions in this book, you will combine Eastern and Western wisdom. The two approaches to psychophysical relaxation combine wonderfully well.

Excellent protection against stress will be afforded by the relaxation response if it is elicited frequently. Dr Benson's research has shown that the effects start to wear off in a few days if a technique for eliciting it is not kept up. Best results come from experiencing the response twice daily, spaced six hours or longer apart. A duration in each session of ten to twenty minutes is adequate. Longer sessions of passive relaxation do not add appreciably to the relaxation effect and are difficult to sustain without distractions becoming obtrusive, mainly from within the mind.

Are there any drawbacks or dangers to the relaxation response? None that I know of. Becoming too passive or too withdrawn a personality is more a danger associated with lack of energy, neuroses, drug or alcohol addiction, certain religious beliefs, and other influences, rather than with the practice of relaxation. The practice of relaxation requires a quiet discipline, sometimes described as 'effortless concentration' in manuals on meditation, and the majority of people practising relaxation find that they have more energy, more alertness, and released faculties of creativity, so that they become more active than before starting training in relaxation. However, they may find that they are choosing *different* areas of activity than before learning to relax well.

Another fear sometimes expressed is that of having strange mental experiences. The relaxation methods described in this book are very unlikely in themselves to lead to hallucinations or any undesirable mental manifestations, unless a predisposition to this is already present before practice begins, or unless the practice of deep relaxation or meditation is continued to lengths well beyond those advocated here, which is ten to twenty minutes' duration, twice daily.

3

Neuromuscular Relaxation

Nervous overactivity and muscle tension

Millions of people in the industrial countries suffer the symptoms of so-called 'nervous tension'. It should be noted that the term 'nervous tension' – though used by doctors as well as by lay persons – is a misnomer. The term refers to nervous overactivity and to the muscle tension it causes. Muscles contract as a result of nerves discharging into them, and can be recorded as electrical activity in the muscles. The subjective experience is as though the nerves have been drawn taut; but it is the muscle fibres and not the nerves that contract. *There is no such thing as nervous tension: only nervous overactivity and muscular tension.* When persons complain of suffering from 'nervous tension', 'nerves', or simply 'tension', nervous excitement and muscle tension is what they mean.

Muscle contraction is part of normal everyday activity: without it our muscles would soon atrophy and become useless. When we refer to 'tension' in this book, it will be in the sense of muscular contraction to a degree in excess of that needed for normal healthy functioning or at a higher level than that required during a session of deep motionless relaxation.

Because of nervous overactivity, many people are unable to relax and release tension in their body muscles even when the conditions for rest are favourable. Dr Edmund Jacobson, the pioneer of progressive relaxation, defines in his book *You Must Relax* 'nervous overactivity' as 'the failure of the individual to be relaxed when and where he should be normally.'

In 1964, an industrial medical officer estimated that British industry lost about eighteen million man hours every year through nervous disorders. The figures for loss of production become astronomical when the loss for all developed countries is thought about. For it does not end there – the obvious nervous disorders are but the tip of an iceberg of psychosomatic ill-health and disease linked with stress. Dr Jacobson wrote his book *Progressive Relaxation* in 1929, in the belief, he says, 'that the universal trend toward overactive minds and bodies could result in various ills.' Subsequent research and clinical experience by himself and other physicians has confirmed this view.

It is a well-known principle of physics, going back to Galileo, that a moving body tends to keep on moving. Overactive people find this is true of themselves when they try to sit or lie motionless. At night, in bed, the eventual attainment of sleep is often the outcome of exhaustion following a struggle against the drive by body and mind to continue activity.

Functional hyperactivity leads to a breakdown. A person can take only so much over-stimulation and over-excitement. Nerves carry signals from the brain to the muscles and also from the muscles to the brain. The greater the nervous stimulation, the more tension there is in the muscles. Emotional stress stimulates tension in the body muscles, whose contractions stimulate further nervous activity.

Muscle relaxation

The most practical way to tackle the problem of nervous overactivity is through the one body system accessible to direct conscious control – the skeletal muscle system. *The vicious circle can be broken by relaxing the muscles and turning down the nervous activity*.

By learning to recognise tension in the body muscles and the face and to let go from it, you can influence the psycho-physical organism as a whole, dissolving muscle tension, quietening the nervous system, and promoting peace of mind. During relaxation the sympathetic branch of the involuntary nervous system is inhibited and the parasympathetic part becomes more active. The sympathetic nervous system is very active in the high arousal state of the fight-or-flight response and the parasympathetic nervous system functions prominently in the low arousal state of the relaxation response. If you keep your muscles relaxed, an alarm reaction is not triggered off so easily, and what before were acute problems are often no longer problems at all, or little ones that are easily coped with. When you are free of excessive electrical excitement in the nervous system, you think more clearly, and sort out problems more easily and effectively.

Electrical activity in the brain varies from mild and rhythmical to powerful excitement with irregular electrical wave patterns. *Muscle tension* keeps the brain excited and activates cells controlling areas of the body other than that originally contracted. Other body systems are aroused. Heart rate, circulation, and blood pressure increase and breathing becomes faster and irregular. *Muscle relaxation* keeps brain activity quiet and rhythmical, with reduced excitement and activity in other body systems. Breathing becomes slower and more even; the heart beats more slowly; electrical excitement in the nervous system is cut down. The nurturing and recuperative processes function well – digestion becomes more efficient, also the replacement of body cells lost through wear and tear.

Progressive relaxation

The close relationship between muscle tension and anxiety has been observed by medical scientists. Edmund Jacobson pioneered research into this relationship and saw the therapeutic lesson that could be learned. He realised that by relaxing skeletal muscles both body and mind would become calmer and excitement responsible both for causing illness and impeding recovery would be cut down and possibly cut out. He developed the system of *progressive relaxation*, in which muscles are relaxed, group by group, throughout the body. Recovery in a variety of physical and mental illnesses was helped (see Chapter 8). And his patients reported how peaceful they felt when they relaxed.

The principle behind learning progressive relaxation is tensing a muscle group and letting go from the tension. You deliberately tense a muscle group and focus your attention on the sensation you feel at that place in your body. The contraction is sustained, and attended to, for five or six seconds. Then you let go from tension and dwell on the feeling of relaxation in the muscles. Thus relaxation becomes a neuromuscular skill that may be learned as you learn other neuromuscular skills, such as walking, buttoning a coat, riding a bicycle, or driving a car.

The trainee's muscle tension is *isometric* – which means that it is a static contraction without movement of the limbs as would occur in training with weights or in sports and games. A static tension aids awareness during relaxation training, whereas movement could be distracting. A whole system of exercise can be isometric and people familiar with isometrics as a fitness programme will have a useful start for training in muscle relaxation: they will know what muscle tension feels like and so be in a position to learn to let go from it. My book, *Isometrics: A Short Cut to Fitness*, gives programmes of head to feet static contraction exercises, and *New Faces* tells how to exercise the facial muscles with isometric contractions. Relaxation of the facial muscles has a key function in calming the mind.

There are muscles to tense and relax associated with *thinking*. These are the muscles of the eyes, connected with imagery, and, very important, the lips, tongue, and other muscles used in speech. Scientific tests show that a large part of thinking is silent speech: sensitive instruments can record the movements of the speech muscles as we think in words. Similarly, in following images in the mind the eye muscles can be detected in their movements and contractions. So progressive neuromuscular relaxation, like meditation, offers us a way to cut down on all that unnecessary mental busyness most of us engage in and to bring stillness and silence into the mind.

The solvent that removes tension from muscles in neuromuscular relaxation is *awareness*. We have a special sense that makes muscle awareness possible. Most adults have allowed it to fall into neglect. The sense whereby you learned to accurately scratch an ear or your nose is called the *kinaesthetic sense*. It is also used to learn more important neuromuscular skills. Training in progressive relaxation sharpens the kinaesthetic sense so that it becomes an instrument for coping well with tension and anxiety, and enjoying the benefits of deep relaxation. In a few weeks most people can become familiar with both tension and relaxation in their skeletal muscles.

Once you have learned the technique of relaxation, you need no longer tense muscles – awareness itself, a sort of unvoiced request to a muscle group to let go, will be effective.

In Dr Jacobson's original method, considerable attention and time is given to one muscle group in each training session, and the whole learning process takes sixty hours. This is a long drawn out procedure for both doctor and patient. Later, other therapists found that *all* groups of muscles could be given attention in a single session and the whole method learned in a few weeks. This shortened version will be taught here. Progressive relaxation can be self-taught, using book instruction, and the procedure is self-directed. Some people find it helpful to make a tape recording of the instructions for playback at training sessions. If you don't like the sound of your own voice, ask another person to make the recording, or do without. As far as possible, sources of distraction or of irritation, however mild, are to be minimised.

The method can be gauged by squeezing one hand into a tight fist for six seconds. Focus attention on the tension in hand and forearm. Now open the hand, let go, and experience the contrasting feeling of relaxation for twelve seconds. The more clearly you focus attention on a muscle group, the better the results.

Progressive neuromuscular relaxation is training in body awareness – how your muscles feel in tension and in relaxation. This awareness is useful in activity throughout the day, as well as in moments of lying or sitting still. Once you have acquired the 'feeling' of muscle relaxation, it can permeate every facet of body–mind activity, waking or even sleeping. The 'feeling' of muscle relaxation is helpful in artistic or sporting performance and is a notable feature of the 'natural performer' in both interests.

Muscle relaxation is the foundation of relaxed living, on which everything else may be built. The simplicity and directness of the method appeals to almost everyone. Obviously, this is basic and essential relaxation training, free from associations that might arouse negative feelings in some people.

Relaxation without trying

Relaxation is a *simple* technique. Paradoxically, the chief difficulty many people have to overcome in learning to relax *is* its simplicity.

Relaxing is *non-doing, letting go from tension*. Relaxation is *an absence of tension* or *manifesting the minimum of tension appropriate in any situation*. Lying flat on one's back or sitting still gives the best opportunities for the deepest muscle relaxation. Minimum tension and maximum relaxation in efficient activity may be called *dynamic relaxation*.

In an achievement- and possession-minded environment, letting go and doing nothing may at first feel strange and unfamiliar; it may even arouse feelings of guilt, either conscious or unconscious. For we are, from an early age, encouraged to be up-and-doing, competing, achieving, go-getting, doing something at all times. So relaxation requires practice by people used to constant activity and who feel guilty at the thought of doing nothing. Most Westerners fall into this category.

A related problem is that most people make the mistake, initially, of *trying* to relax. This is as counterproductive an approach as trying to sleep. Relaxation, like sleep, is attained through an *indirect* approach. You concern yourself with means rather than with ends. Instead of thinking of relaxation, and trying to relax, you should follow with full attention and clear awareness the sequence of letting go in each muscle group throughout the body. Relaxation comes to you indirectly. The *letting go* is the relaxation. You see, it really is very simple. Whoever you are and wherever you are, as Walt Whitman used to address his readers, you can release tension and relax.

Two relaxation programmes

In *Programme One* you spend a minimum of four weeks in daily – or better twice daily – practice of tension-release. You become aware of tension – then of absence of tension, which is relaxation – in this muscle, that muscle or muscle group, until you have focussed attention on the whole body and the face. We include muscles used in imagery and in inner speech, so that peace of mind becomes a neuromuscular skill.

The principle behind this tense-and-let-go training of Programme One may be restated briefly. Because most adults have lost touch with the feelings of tension and of relaxation in their skeletal muscles, it is necessary to train the kinaesthetic or muscle-awareness sense to greater efficiency. You must be aware of tension in a muscle before you can let go from it. Awareness of muscle tension, awareness of absence of tension – that is the learning method of Programme One. Just as we can enjoy and be more aware of the warmth of an open fire immediately after clearing a front garden path of snow, so we learn to feel and to enjoy muscle relaxation if it immediately follows deliberate muscle tension. The contrast between the two states promotes deep relaxation. Later, when we have good mind–muscle rapport, we no longer need to deliberately tense muscles and muscle groups to promote passive relaxation.

In practising *Programme Two* you let your attention dwell on parts of the body and the facial muscles in the same sequence that was followed in Programme One, but now there is no need to contract any muscles; you simply let your trained awareness deal with tension in any muscle group. You relax from toes to head, without any muscle movements and without talking to yourself inwardly.

As pointed out earlier, from the start we will be relaxing *all* the main body muscles and the facial muscles in each session. In Jacobson's original training programme you would spend all the time in a session giving attention to one body part, learning to tense and release another body part on another day. This is no longer felt to be necessary, and there will be here an opportunity for head-to-toe relaxation at every training session.

Another point worth repeating is that the method of tensing muscles before letting go from tension is a *temporary* training method, which can be dropped once its task has been completed, though some people may like to use it occasionally, as a reminder of what letting go is all about. Once you have learned to recognise muscle tension, a sensitivity which probably had become blunted, you can directly play the torch beam of your attention on a muscle or muscle group, and release tension! Most people can make this change – from practising Programme One to practising Programme Two as set out in this book – in four to six weeks. But continue the contraction exercises for a few days or weeks longer if you do not feel ready to give them up. You may find it helpful to make a gradual transition, using Programme One at a first relaxation session of a day, and Programme Two at a second session. When you feel ready for it, drop Programme One and stay with Programme Two thereafter.

A further point worth making is that eventually you should be able to speed up the process of relaxation. Your honed awareness will make it possible for you to relax by sweeping your attention smoothly and rapidly over your muscles and turning on relaxed awareness. But fast relaxation is a reward for earlier training.

About the sequence
The words 'progressive relaxation' refer to programmes of relaxation based on relaxing body muscles and muscle groups sequentially. There is a certain logic to the sequence. It is usual to move from feet to head or from head to feet, letting go in adjacent muscle groups. But some variation occurs in sequence according to the preferences of individual teachers. These differences are of only minor significance; what is really important is that all the body parts have an opportunity to release tension. Until recently, I have tended to favour a straight sequence of moving up the body from feet to head – giving attention, in turn, to lower legs, upper legs, buttocks, abdomen, back, chest; then the arms from hands to shoulders; finally relaxing the facial muscles from the neck to the scalp. The difference in sequence I follow now is only very slightly changed. We use our hands and arms so much in our conscious efforts, that I now like to start the programmes by directing attention to the dominant arm, then to the other arm, and then moving attention up the legs to the head. The change from my earlier sequence is merely a matter of psychological nuance, and nothing more significant than that is claimed for it.

The muscles and muscle groups to be relaxed are listed below in order of attention. Let your gaze move down the list a few times, accompanying the reading of each line with brief awareness of the body part named.

Muscles and muscle groups to be relaxed in sequence

1   Hands
2   Forearms
3   Front upper arms (biceps)
4   Rear upper arms (triceps)
5   Feet
6   Front lower legs (shins)
7   Rear lower legs (calves)
8   Front upper legs (thigh extensors)
9   Rear upper legs (thigh biceps)

10   Buttocks
11   Abdomen
12   Lower back
13   Upper back
14   Chest
15   Shoulders
16   Neck
17   Throat
18   Jaw
19   Lips
20   Tongue
21   Eyes
22   Forehead and scalp
23   Imagery muscles ⎫
24   Speech muscles ⎬ thinking muscles

Surroundings and conditions conducive to passive relaxation
Perhaps one day you will be able to relax in a noisy crowded place, but in early training in relaxation you should seek to minimise distractions in the physical environment. To some extent there is individual variation in what may prove distracting in surroundings.

Select a quiet place, with subdued lighting.

Best results come from practising at fixed times each day. Most people practise passive relaxation at home, though one or two daily sessions could be at an office or other place of employment.

The room should have a comfortable temperature and be free from either stuffiness or draughts.

The room should also be free from unpleasant associations – 'bad vibrations', as some people say – or objects that trigger feelings not conducive to relaxation, such as irritation, embarrassment, or guilt. In short, find an harmonious place to relax.

Be alone. Even two is a 'crowd' when it comes to starting to learn to relax well.

Wash at least your hands and face. 'Freshening up' in itself starts the process of releasing tension.

Empty your bladder; a full bladder would be a distraction. Empty your bowels, also, if this should be a pressing problem. Any body sensations that would disrupt muscle awareness should be eliminated as far as possible.

Wear comfortable clothing, nothing tight that could set up tensions and draw your attention away from detecting muscle tensions. Unbutton shirt collars, waistcoats. Remove shoes, spectacles, contact lenses, ties, belts, anything likely to be constricting or distracting.

Remember that you will be lying motionless for ten to twenty minutes, so make sure that you are not going to become chilled.

The surroundings and conditions conducive to passive relaxation that have been described above contribute to the *right attitude* for teaching yourself to relax well, which is to feel open, aware, and loose to life.

Lying-on-back position
Lying flat on your back with your legs and arms extended and every part of the body having even base support is the best position for letting go and learning awareness relaxation. Relaxation sitting in a chair should be added later.

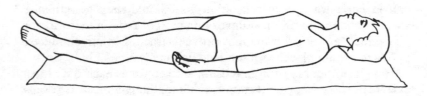

If you lie on the floor, have a rug or folded blanket beneath you. A floor provides firm even support, but cover the surface for some comfort, otherwise after some minutes the hardness of the floor will start becoming a distraction. The alternative is a couch or firm bed – too yielding a surface sets up tensions in the skeletal muscles and prevents an even distribution of body weight. A gymnasium mat gives excellent support.

Lie flat on your back, with your legs and arms outstretched limply. Your heels may be apart a few inches, and the feet falling limply to either side. Your legs should feel loose (not locked) at the knees, and your arms should feel loose (not locked) at the elbows. The arms may be bent very slightly at the elbows.

Your arms should be extended alongside, but a little out from, the sides of your body. Having the hands lie limply about one foot away from the hips feels 'right' for most people, but it is not a matter of being inch perfect. The best positions for your hands are with the palms facing inwards and slightly up, each thumb resting on an index finger. Your hands should feel limp, like empty gloves.

Your head should be central between your shoulders and neither twisted nor tilted in any direction; if you opened your eyes during the relaxation session you would be looking directly upwards. However, you should keep your eyes closed lightly; closing the eyes is known to favour the appearance of alpha waves in the brain, a pattern of electrical activity associated with relaxation.

Your weight should be supported evenly at all points of contact – back of head, shoulders, upper back, lower back, buttocks, backs of thighs, calves, heels; the upper arms, the elbows, forearms, and hands. Feel good contact and support at every point and make the necessary slight adjustments in position to give an even distribution of body weight. You should feel that you are able to let go and rest with your full weight – like a sleeping baby or cat!

If you feel discomfort in the lower back, it is most likely to be because the psoas muscle, an unfamiliar name to most people, is being pulled tight by the extended legs. The psoas muscle travels from the base of the spine to the tops of the thigh bones, passing through the abdomen; the outstretched legs can tighten the muscle so that it pulls on the lower back, causing an uncomfortable, even painful feeling. Placing small cushions under the thighs so as to bend the knees will usually take care of lower back discomfort, because the psoas muscle slackens.

There may also be a postural fault, the lower back not flattening down on the base surface. Postural practice standing against a wall will help overcome this.

If pressure on the back of your head becomes a distraction, a pillow, cushion, or pad of soft material may be placed behind the head and neck.

Just as later you should be able to relax with more distractions in the physical environment to cope with, so in time you should be able to lie or sit and relax even though there is some initial discomfort. Some teachers of relaxation – the Australian psychiatrist Dr Ainslie Meares, for example – take the view that it is excellent training to relax while experiencing slight discomfort and so learn to transcend it; but most experts in relaxation recommend maximum freedom from all possible distractions, at least in early practice.

Some people when learning relaxation while lying on the back pass into sleep. Teachers giving relaxation instruction to groups are familiar with the sound of snoring coming from one or two parts of the room when the pupils are lying on the floor. The sleep is likely to be of good quality, but sleeping is not relaxing. If you do sleep for a few minutes, on awakening you should recommence the programme at the last point you can recall. If sleeping becomes habitual during training, then sitting is a better relaxation position than lying on the back.

Deep muscle relaxation can be achieved while sitting comfortably, but most people will make fastest progress by learning first to let go from tension while lying down. Programme One may be undertaken while sitting in one daily relaxation session after three or four weeks of tense-and-let-go training lying down, using Programme Two in recumbent position for the other session of the day. The practice of Programme Two while sitting can follow three weeks daily training in Programme One while sitting.

You may find that you are most comfortable in the type of armchair in which you can recline with your legs extended. This is suitable for use for relaxation practice providing the back of your head is supported. Your feet may rest on their outer edges, soles facing. This foot position may also be used, with the legs more bent at the knees, in certain contour chairs. In some chairs it may be necessary to place a small cushion against the lower back for a stable posture that is free from spinal strain. Remember that you will be sitting motionless in Programme Two for up to twenty minutes and not be moving most of the time in Programme One. Both programmes may also be practised sitting in poised posture, head and trunk in vertical line, as described on pages 73–5. This is also a sound posture for the practice of meditation (Chapter 7). If you rest your wrists on the tops of your thighs, your hands may be held with palms facing and slightly up, and the fingers of one hand may lightly touch those of the other hand.

Take opportunities as they present themselves to let go from tension in your musculature (Programme Two) while sitting watching television, listening to the radio or music on record, on train or bus, in a dentist's or doctor's waiting room, and so on. It is even possible to relax considerably while reading, especially if you use a book rest. A combination of poised-posture sitting and minimum muscular contraction is always helpful in keeping the nervous system calm and in conserving energy.

Programme One

Lie on your back in the supine starting position described above.

Before commencing the tense-and-let-go conditioning controls, there are three things you can do to help create the right mood, attitude, and body state for relaxation training. The first is to stretch like a cat for a few seconds; the second is to close your eyes lightly; and the third is to be aware of your breathing for a minute or two.

Cat stretching
This promotes a feeling of fresh and open awareness. It also initiates the process of releasing muscle tension.

While in the lying on back position . . . S–T–R–E–T–C–H with cat-like enjoyment. Stretch for about ten seconds and enjoy every second of it. Think of your body as having two halves: above and below the waist. Stretch downwards with the lower half and the arms, as though attempting to elongate your legs, hips, lower abdomen, and arms. Keep your heels in contact with the base surface, but your arms may lose contact and be slightly raised. Your arms will pull your shoulders downwards. Simultaneously, stretch your head and upper body in the opposite direction to the legs, pelvis, and arms. You will feel as if your neck and trunk muscles above the waist are lengthening; but keep your shoulders pulled down by your arms.

Take a deep breath before starting the cat stretch and let it out like a long heartfelt sigh during it.

Finally, *let go* . . . feet and legs, hands and arms, trunk, neck, and face . . . let all your muscles go limp.

Make any last adjustments to your position, in the light of the description given above of the best supine or sitting position for relaxation. Be aware of even contact with the base surface and of the other requirements for a good relaxation posture. Having made the final adjustments to your posture, you stay in the one position for the whole of the programme.

Close your eyes
The next thing to do is to close your eyes. Don't squeeze and screw up your face; let the lids lower slowly and stay down lightly. In doing this you are cutting out distracting visual stimuli, and promoting slow alpha wave activity in the brain. And with your eyes closed, it becomes easier to focus attention on your muscles in sequence.

Awareness of breathing
For two to three minutes, before starting to contract and relax muscles, be aware of your breathing, in particular of the expansion and contraction of the breathing muscles, which are those of the thorax, diaphragm, and abdomen.

There is a method of breathing which is conducive to deep relaxation, and also to good health. Cultivate it now, and it will do more than help you relax; it will improve your health and heighten your sense of well-being. Moreover, awareness of breathing in this manner will be helpful for the practice of meditation, as described in Chapter 7.

The supine position for deep relaxation encourages diaphragmatic–abdominal breathing, which is the most healthful breathing mode.

Shallow, high, upper-chest breathing is an inadequate method of breathing that is associated with slumped or rigid postures and with states of anxiety and tension. On the other hand, diaphragmatic–abdominal breathing is associated with poised posture, in which all the breathing muscles have freedom to act, and with states of calm and relaxation.

Be aware of the action of the respiratory muscles when you allow them to function freely and to take air deep down into the lungs. If you are guilty of shallow high-chest breathing, you should practise diaphragmatic–abdominal breathing for a few minutes several times in a day until the most healthful breathing action becomes habitual. In it, the thorax expands and the large dome-shaped diaphragm, situated above the navel, flattens out and moves down on breathing in. On breathing out, the thorax contracts and the diaphragm ascends and resumes its dome shape. The abdominal wall is massaged by this piston-like activity of the diaphragm – it swells out on breathing in and falls back on breathing out. Be aware of the rise and fall of the abdominal wall as you lie on your back, as well as the activity of the thorax and diaphragm; the supine supported position favours clear awareness of diaphragmatic–abdominal breathing, though it can also be sensed in a sitting posture.

Note well the muscular sensations of diaphragmatic–abdominal breathing and remember to breathe in this way at other times of the day: when sitting, when active, and when lying in bed and about to go to sleep. In short, practise this healthful and relaxing mode of breathing until it becomes habitual.

If you have not yet become familiar with diaphragmatic–abdominal breathing, you will find it helpful, as you lie on your back in the relaxation position, to bend your arms and rest the palms of your hands on your abdomen so that the tips of your longest fingers touch together just over your navel. Let the backs of your upper arms rest on the base surface and tuck your forearms in against your ribs. You will then clearly feel the action of the lower ribs against the forearms, thrusting against the arms as you breathe in, while the diaphragm is felt to move down and raise the belly beneath your hands. The reverse action accompanies the exhalation of breath. Be aware of the activity of the breathing muscles during five or six inhalations and exhalations with your hands on your abdomen, then return your hands and arms to the starting position.

Awareness of breathing follows the cat stretch and should continue for two to three minutes. It gets muscle awareness under way. Don't interfere with your breathing in any way. Don't force air in or out of your lungs; *letting it happen* is the right attitude to take. You will find that as relaxation deepens your rate of breathing slows down, and the breathing movement becomes smoother and more rhythmical. Fast and jerky breathing is associated with tension and emotional excitement. Slow and smooth breathing is associated with states of relaxation and emotional calm.

Occasional involuntary large in-breaths and out-breaths during deep relaxation are not uncommon; muscle twitches also may occur now and then. Both are natural occurrences. When breathing becomes slow, there may build up a need for a compensating large breath. The muscle twitches are a sign of a discharge of tension-energy in a muscle.

After being passively aware of the sensations evoked by the spontaneous activity of your respiratory muscles, which is itself enough to start the process of quietening and slowing down our body–mind organism, you are then ready to start the tense-and-let-go training.

Tense and let go
In Programme One, which is a relaxation training programme, you tense and let go in a sort of wordless dialogue between you and your skeletal muscles. Each muscle or muscle group receives your full attention as it is tensed for a duration of six seconds. If you practise counting inwardly 'one, two, three, four, five, six' while looking at the moving second hand on a watch or clock, you will learn quickly to measure mentally the six-second interval. The same method takes care of the interval of twelve seconds during which you are fully aware of the feeling of relaxation – letting go from tension – which follows each contraction. The time given to awareness of relaxation in a muscle is twice that given to awareness of contraction.

Perfection in timing is not asked for; to do so would be more likely to create anxiety than relaxation. Spend a few minutes with a watch or clock, becoming familiar with the six and the twelve second intervals and thereafter this aspect of the training programme need not trouble you.

Right attitude
The principle behind tensing muscles and letting go from tension has already been made clear. However, a few words may be helpful about the right approach or attitude you bring to practice, even if this means repeating points made earlier.

Tense and be aware of tension. Let go and be aware of relaxation. The very simplicity of the practice is an obstacle that may have to be overcome. The tension gives you something to let go from. It is necessary to repeat that in letting go no effort is called for – this is *non-doing*. Passive awareness itself effects the change to deepening relaxation. Therefore, the right attitude may be summarised as 'let it happen'. If you observe the muscles passively, they will relax.

American relaxation expert Joseph Kennedy said that the 'secret' of successful relaxation technique was to concentrate on means rather than on ends. This means that you concentrate fully on each stage of the programme and let the overall goal of body–mind relaxation come as it will. If you give full attention to one muscle or muscle group, then move on to the next, the muscles that previously received the light of awareness will go on relaxing.

Awareness is fully switched on, but no effort is called for. Don't *try* to relax. Let it come indirectly. One of the two main schools of Zen Buddhism call their practice of meditation 'just sitting meditation'. We can make use of the 'just' idea for right attitude for relaxation. Just tense, just let go. Just direct your attention to this muscle, that muscle, in sequence. Just be aware of whatever stage you have reached in the programme. Catch the simplicity of what you do and don't do.

This is the best I can do to describe something which must be experienced to be understood. The words are not the experience. Fortunately, right awareness is not difficult to experience and once known may be brought thereafter to each relaxation session, whether of Programme One or of Programme Two. This training in attention-awareness will prove a great value when it comes to your learning meditation for relaxation (Chapter 7), as well as in all aspects of day-to-day living.

Final points
Remember to stay aware (passively, without forcing) of the feeling of tension as you contract each muscle or muscle group for six seconds, and be equally aware of the contrasting feeling of relaxation, for twelve seconds, after you let go from the contraction. Relaxation is the letting go, a non-doing following a doing (tensing). The muscles go limp. You let relaxation happen.

Breathe gently through your nostrils during the programme when not contracting muscles. During a contraction awareness of the sensation of tension will be aided by holding your breath or controlling your breathing so that it is barely perceptible.

Let your attention move from muscle group to muscle group in sequence like a torch beam resting on one object, then another, in a dark room.

The sequence as given starts with the right hand, but left-handed people may start with their left hand, which is the one they are most familiar with using.

In practice, the sequence of muscle controls is logical and quickly memorised, but a concise key to the relaxation-conditioning movements follows for guidance in the early stages of learning to recognise tension and to let go from it.

Devote twenty minutes to each of the two programmes.

Concise key to the conditioning movements

No.	To contract the	Movement
1	hand	bend up fingers
		make tight fist
2	wrist and forearm	bend up hand
3	front upper arm (biceps)	flex arm
4	rear upper arm (triceps)	straighten arm
5	foot	bend up toes
6	ankle and front lower leg (shin)	bend up foot
7	rear lower leg (calf)	point toes
8	front upper leg (thigh extensors)	straighten leg
9	rear upper leg (thigh biceps)	pull heel back
10	buttocks	tighten
11	abdomen	flatten abdominal wall
12	lower back	arch spine
13	upper back	shoulders back and in
14	chest	shoulders forward and in
15	shoulders	shrug
16	neck	press back head
17	throat	press chin on to chest
18	jaw	clench teeth
19	lips	press lips together
20	tongue	teeth together, press tongue against roof of mouth
21	eyes	look right, left, up, down
		squeeze tightly shut
22	forehead and scalp	frown
23	imagery muscles	visualise scene
24	speech muscles	think verbally

Arms

Lying down or sitting comfortably, breathing gently and evenly, your relaxation training programme starts by directing your attention to your arms: hand, wrist, forearm, and upper arm, front and back. If you are left-handed, you may feel more comfortable tensing and relaxing your left hand first, then your right hand, and so on.

Right hand: (*a*) Having turned down the palm of your right hand and keeping the palm and heel of the hand firmly down, raise your fingers up and back towards your wrists. Keep your fingers straight. They will not rise or come back very far, but the contraction of the back of the hand will be strongly felt. Stay aware of the sensation of tension in the hand for six seconds. Then let go, the fingers flopping down. Return the hand to its starting position and become aware of the hand as limp and loose, like an empty glove. Be aware of tension in the hand for six seconds and of relaxation for twelve seconds. Three gentle calm breaths may be about right. Six seconds contracting, twelve seconds being aware of letting go applies throughout the programme. Use this timing in each of the tense-and-let-go exercises.

(*b*) Squeeze your hand into a hard, tight fist. Note the tension in the hand, particularly in the frontal surfaces. Contract the hand only: all other body parts and the facial muscles should be at rest. Then let go, unwinding the fingers into the starting position. Think of the hand going loose and limp. Be aware of the contrast between this sensation and the preceding tension.

Your right hand (or left hand if you are left-handed) puts in a lot of work, and it is important to be able to relax it. And clenched fists are perhaps the most familiar manifestation of angry or excitable states.

Left hand: Repeat the (*a*) and (*b*) contractions with the left hand: lifting the fingers up and back and making a hard fist respectively.

Right wrist and forearm: Turn palm down, straightening fingers. Keeping wrist and forearm firmly down, raise all of your hand up and back against the wrist joint. As the hand comes up you will feel lines of tension run up the arm from wrist to elbow. Keep the hand hard up against the wrist joint for the usual six seconds, then lower and relax the hand, returning it to its original position. Keep attention-awareness on the resting wrist and forearm for twelve seconds or three slow calm breaths.

Left wrist and forearm: Raise your left hand up and back against your wrist and stay aware of the contraction of the wrist and forearm, then of the relaxation in the same parts when you have lowered your hand and allowed it to go limp.

Right upper arm (*biceps*): This is the muscle the professional strongman is always contracting, which he does by flexing an arm, bringing the fist up to the shoulder. Turn up the palm of your right hand. Without altering the position of your upper arm, make a fist and bring it up slowly to your right shoulder, causing the biceps muscle to bunch and harden. Be aware of this biceps contraction, also its relaxation after you have lowered your right hand to the starting position.

Left upper arm (*biceps*):   Flex your left arm as you did the right arm, and then allow it to go limp. Take good note of the sensation of tension and of relaxation. The biceps' function is to flex the arm.

Right upper arm (*triceps*):   This is the three-headed muscle at the back of the upper arm, whose function is to straighten the arm. Use the final contraction position of the preceding control, arm flexed, fist at shoulder. Slowly straighten the arm until it has locked at the elbow. Feel the strong contraction on the underside of the upper arm. Let go from it, feeling the elbow joint and the triceps go loose. Stay aware of the feeling of letting go for the required time.

Left upper arm (*triceps*):   Contract the left triceps and be fully aware of the sensation; then of the resulting relaxation when you let go from the contraction and allow the arm to go limp.

Checking: You have reached a point for checking on your relaxation progress. Let your attention travel up your right arm (left arm if you are left-handed) from hand to shoulder. There may be a comfortable feeling of heaviness and/or warmth, with perhaps some tingling. These are sensations of progress. If you have feelings of heaviness or warmth, these may be encouraged by giving yourself suggestions of their intensifying. Such sensations are a natural development as you become more aware of muscle sensations. There is less tension; circulation is improving; the blood vessels are opening more; the muscles are becoming less resistant, more soft, limp, and loose. The arm feels better supported by bed, couch, floor, or ground. It feels as though it has expanded. There are, however, individual variations in how relaxation is experienced. Take about twelve seconds for each passive awareness of the segments of the arm that were contracted and relaxed. Give similar attention-awareness to the left (or right) arm, hand, wrist and forearm, front upper arm, rear upper arm. Feel the relaxation spreading from the upper arms into the shoulder caps.

Legs
Now move your beam of attention to your legs, which contain some powerful muscles. The sequence here is foot, ankle and shin, calf,

thigh extensors (front upper leg) and thigh biceps (back upper leg). If it feels more natural to you – if, say, you play football and kick most powerfully with your left foot – start with your left foot, the reverse of the description given here.

Right foot: Let your attention dwell on your right foot. (*a*) Without moving the rest of your foot, curl up your toes. Feel the tension on the upper surface of the foot. Take note of them, also the relaxation when the toes are released to take their most restful position.

(*b*) Curl your toes in strongly towards the sole of the foot, contracting it. Observe the contraction and the relaxation when the toes become limp again.

Left foot: Perform the (*a*) and (*b*) toe curls, up and down respectively. Again be alertly but passively aware of the tensions in the top and sole of the foot.

Right ankle and front lower leg (*shin*):   Raise the whole of your right foot up against the ankle joint as far as it will go, keeping the rest of your leg steady. Feel the lines of tension in the front lower leg. Be aware of tension. Let the foot move back to its most comfortable position. Note the contrasting relaxation. It is important to be on guard against contracting muscles, to any degree, away from the area of the conditioning control. For example, in moving your foot up and back, you should not contract your hand or jaw.

Left ankle and front lower leg (*shin*):   Raise your left foot up and back against the ankle joint. Be aware of the tension in the front lower leg and the ankle joint. Let the foot go back to the relaxed position. Be aware of the relaxation.

Right rear lower leg (*calf*):   Point your right foot strongly away from the rest of the body contracting the calf muscle at the rear of the lower leg. If the calf starts cramping, stop at once, rest a minute or so, then perform the control again, less hard the next time. Let the foot return to its natural position, relaxed and moving out a little to the right side. The calf muscle now feels loose and floppy. Be aware of the feeling in the calf.

Left rear lower leg (*calf*):   Contract the left calf by stretching the left foot away from you. Let go after six seconds and note how the calf feels as though it is hanging limply from the lower leg bone.

Right front upper leg (*thigh extensors*):   The thighs are very powerful muscles, especially the extensors which extend or straighten the leg. We can straighten our legs with very heavy loads on our shoulders and backs. To contract the extensors, raise your knee a little, bending the leg and drawing your heel back a few inches. Now straighten your leg fully, locking it at the knee joint, and contract the top of your thigh so that the shortened muscle fibres become hard and bunched together, as those on the back of your upper arm did earlier when you straightened your arm. Now let your thigh muscles go slack and at rest. Observe their relaxation. Let go from tension.

Left front upper leg (*thigh extensors*):   Contract and relax the muscles which extend your left leg. Closely be aware of the muscles contracting as you straighten your leg and of the muscles going slack as you release the contraction.

Right rear upper leg (*thigh biceps*):   Bending your right leg, raise your knee a few inches and press the heel of your foot down and back against bed, couch, floor, or ground, which provides the immovable resistance that produces a static or isometric contraction of the biceps of the thigh. Just as the arm biceps flexes the arm, the thigh biceps flexes the thigh. A blocked movement is the principle of isometric contraction exercise. The contraction of the muscles at the back of the upper leg should be unmistakable. This exercise is unfamiliar to most people, so be on guard against pressing too hard and producing a painful cramp in early sessions. Stop instantly if cramp is imminent, rest a minute or so, then repeat the control, more gently this time. Following awareness of the contraction of the thigh biceps, let the whole leg go limp, and extend the leg comfortably into the starting position. Observe the contrasting feeling of relaxation in the rear thigh.

Left rear upper leg (*thigh biceps*):   Bend the left leg, raising the knee a few inches, and press down and back with the heel of the left foot, contracting the muscles at the back of the thigh. Note the contraction; lower the knee and let go from the contraction; be aware of the limp and loose feeling in the thigh.

Checking: Time now to check on how well you have been learning to let go from tension in your legs. Move attention-awareness up your right leg – foot, shin, calf, front thigh, rear thigh. Pause for about twelve seconds on each part and let go from any tension that may still be there. Remember that relaxation is a non-doing. Simply let go. Give similar attention to the muscles of the left leg from foot to thigh. Think of heaviness and/or warmth if it is helpful.

Buttocks and trunk

Buttocks: This is primarily a muscle control and a clear example of the way in which specific groups of muscles may be contracted by directing a message to them. In this case there are two commands of equal importance: 'contract' and 'let go'. The squeezing in of the buttocks may be aided by stretching your legs a little and by tilting your pelvis forward a little. The ease with which we can all perform this muscle control is connected with the skills we learned in childhood in controlling our evacuatory processes. Experts in muscle control can contract and relax at will muscles over which most people have no conscious control.

The genital muscles are also contracted when the buttocks are squeezed in hard. Women attending ante-natal classes may be instructed to tighten their buttocks and squeeze all the parts between their legs together; to hold the contraction for a few seconds; then to let go and let the parts spread and relax. Another technique is to alternately check and release the flow of water when urinating. By practising these muscle controls a woman learns to recognise when she is tensing the muscles of the lower abdomen and pelvic area and when she is relaxing them. The ability to relax the area is important at the stage of labour contractions. Easy breathing is another aid, and thinking of tension flowing out of body and mind on exhaling in an effortless sighing manner.

Abdomen: Dr Jacobson and some other writers on progressive relaxation instruct at this point that the abdominal muscles be pulled back towards the spine. Resistance is met if this is done on full lungs, a practice hardly desirable; otherwise the abdominal wall may be fully relaxed on being drawn back, providing no guide to recognising tension. If (as much as possible) the lungs are emptied of air and the abdomen is kept fully relaxed, the abdominal wall will involuntarily move back into the thoracic cavity – the muscle control called *uddiyani* in Hatha Yoga.

For the reasons given in the preceding paragraph, I recommend, if you are lying down, that you contract your abdomen by bringing your shoulders up and forward as though going to sit up, but without lifting the centre of your back away from its support. At the same time, use mind–muscle control of the kind used to tighten the buttocks – the thought should be 'flatten and harden', with an appropriate visualisation of what is required. If you are sitting upright, it will be necessary to rely on developing mind–muscle control to contract the abdominal wall. An imaginative ploy makes this muscle control instantly understandable and effective: *tense the abdominal wall as though stoically taking a blow to it.*

This is a useful muscle-toning exercise, but our purpose again is to study the sensation of tension in a contracted body part and to become aware of what it feels like when the same group of muscles is relaxed.

It is important to learn to relax the abdomen, for it is an area easily disturbed by fear, anxiety, and other emotions connected with the alarm or fight-or-flight response, causing such familiar sensations as a 'churning stomach' or 'butterflies in the stomach'.

Lower back: Shift your attention to the lower back. The more you relax it, the more it will flatten against the surface on which you are lying or against which you are sitting, though postural faults will in some instances prevent this fully happening.

Become aware of tensions in the lower back by arching your spine, keeping your pelvis and shoulders firmly down. Sustain the contraction for the usual six seconds, then lower your backbone to its former resting position and be aware of letting go from tension.

Upper back: The muscles covering the shoulder blades give the impression of being broad wings. The upper back feels tense when the wings are squeezed in and the back made narrower. Do this now and be aware of the feeling of tension the control engenders. Then, after six seconds, let the upper back broaden again, feel loose, expansive, and relaxed. The shoulders, too, will seem to have spread outwards, and something of the relaxed expansion will be communicated to the lower back.

Chest: To contract the muscles of the upper back you took your shoulders back and squeezed in the shoulder blades. To contract the chest muscles, think of the opposite action. Take your shoulders forward and narrow the chest as much as possible, squeezing in the muscles of the chest, so that they feel as if they are being bunched in the centre of the breast bone. Suspend breathing during the contraction. Compress your chest muscles while rounding your back. Then let go and return your shoulders to their full resting position. Note the relaxation of the chest muscles and the freedom from restriction on breathing.

Shoulders: While keeping the other parts of your body free from contractions, shrug your shoulders up to your ears. Feel the tension across your shoulders. Only your shoulders should have moved. Take care not to tense your neck or upper back. Having noted the tension, allow the shoulders to drop right down. Relaxed shoulders hang low and the arms seem to dangle from them.

Checking: Check unhurriedly but rather briefly that your arms and legs have stayed relaxed. In making some of the contractions of the trunk muscles, one group or more of the arm or leg muscles may have tensed involuntarily. Look for tension and if you detect it, let go from it. After that, let your attention dwell for about twelve seconds on each group of trunk muscles that you tensed and relaxed. Your buttocks should feel loose and your abdomen feel free to gently rise and fall in diaphragmatic–abdominal breathing. Your thorax should feel comfortably expanded and free to make its small contribution to your quiet breathing. If your breathing is gentle, quiet, smooth, and regular, it is a sign of advanced relaxation. If you should take a large breath involuntarily, which may sometimes happen, don't resist it; let the respiratory muscles expand, and think of any residual tension flowing out with your exhaled breath. So useful is this exercise that it is worth doing it now, at this point in your checking for tension in your trunk muscles. Tune in to the natural rhythm of your breathing and without interfering with it, think of tension leaving your body and mind on the next three in–out breaths. Finally, check that your back feels expanded and your shoulders feel loose and wide. Think of heaviness and/or warmth, if the thought is helpful.

Neck

The neck is a body part which frequently registers so-called 'nervous tension'. Other people are often the problem; they can literally become 'pains in the neck'. Fanatics, political or religious, noticeably often have rigid necks. Conversely, there is a connection, which should not be overlooked, between relaxation and the most healthy and expansive attitudes and beliefs.

To become aware of tension in your neck muscles, press your head back against the surface on which you are lying or the back of a chair on which you are sitting. If you are sitting upright with your head unsupported, raise one hand and place the palm across the back of your head: press your head back but prevent any movement of your head with counterpressure from your hand; this produces a static contraction of the neck muscles. Let go, returning your hand to the starting position. When relaxed, your neck should feel as though it has become more soft and supple.

Throat: Press your chin down firmly on to the top of your chest. Be aware of the contraction in the throat muscles. Raise your chin to the level position and allow the throat to become loose and relaxed.

Face
All the contracting and relaxing of muscles that has gone before should have prepared you well for learning to relax the facial muscles, the last group to be tensed and relaxed and probably the most important. They are so important because of the intimate connection between them and your feelings. Their controlled relaxation affords a practical way of inducing mental calm, and of gaining control over harmful emotions. The facial muscles reflect our feelings. Anxiety, fear, anger and their derivative feelings cause facial muscles to compress and distort. On the other hand, feelings of calmness, contentment, serenity, tranquillity, love, and so on are reflected in the face by expansion and relaxation.

Another association between the muscles of the face and the mind worth pointing out is that most people if asked to locate their sense of 'I', of a presiding ego, answer that it is, without any doubt, felt to be in the head. Egoistic striving and straining will become visible in tensions in the facial muscles. The person who is skilled in letting go from tension in the facial muscles – the jaw, mouth, eyes, forehead and scalp – will be in a position to consciously promote a tranquil state of mind and to become aware of and avoid un-necessary mental effort: frowning when concentrating on a mental problem, staring to try and see better, straining to hear better, and so on.

The ability to recognise tension in these muscles and to let go from it is enhanced by exercising them. These muscles – the most subtle and extraordinary we possess, combining strength and deli-cacy to a unique degree – may be exercised through a programme of static (isometric) contractions, firming and toning the face, and with a positive influence on the personality. A programme of this kind can be found in my book *New Faces*.

The exercises for the face given below are all isometric contractions.

Jaw: At times of stress, many people press their upper and lower teeth together, tightening their jaw muscles. That is what you should do now at this stage in the relaxation training programme. Clench your teeth firmly for six seconds, fully aware of the rigidity of your jaw muscles. Let go from the tension, so that your jaw relaxes and your teeth and lips are parted slightly. Concentrate on the feeling of slackness (absence of tension) in the jaw right up to our temples. Remember the sensation both of tension and of relaxation in this part of the face, and remember hereafter to let the first signs of jaw tension be a signal to relax these and other muscles of the face.

Lips: Press your lips together as though struggling not to say something you shouldn't say but would like to. Keep up the pressure for six seconds, noting the tension around the mouth, then let the lips go loose and free for a further twelve seconds of attention-awareness.

Tongue: Bring your upper and lower teeth lightly together. Now curl up your tongue and press it up and back against the roof of your mouth. Be aware of the sensation of contraction in the tongue, followed by the feeling of relaxation when the contraction has been ended and your tongue rests flat in the bottom of your mouth with its tip behind your lower teeth.

Eyes: (*a*) You can become familiar with the feeling of tension in the six small muscles which move the eyeballs by keeping your head immobile but swinging your eyes as far to the right as possible, then as far as possible to the left, as far above, as far below. You do not need to open your eyes to perform this exercise, but if you imagine a clock face in front of your face, you will be looking three o'clock, nine o'clock, twelve o'clock, and six o'clock. At each limit of the eyes' movement, be aware of the tension experienced for six seconds.

(*b*) Now bring your eyebrows hard down and squeeze your eyes tightly shut for six seconds. Let go, so that the eyes are again only lightly shut. Feel the relaxation in and around the eyes. Note how the eyes feel as though they have fallen back and settled comfortably in their sockets: tense people stare and thrust their eyes forward. Could it be that the eyes are also now further apart? That is how it feels. Your temples should feel smooth and peaceful, the opposite of tense and throbbing.

Forehead and scalp: The *occipito frontalis* is a muscle which starts above the eyebrows and extends beneath the scalp over the top of the head to the back of the skull. You can learn to recognise tension in the forehead and scalp and contrasting relaxation by frowning fiercely, wrinkling and squeezing in the forehead and tugging at the scalp. The tension created by this muscle control – a remarkable achievement, mind controlling muscle – is unmistakable. Sustain it for six seconds, then let go and feel the relaxation for twelve seconds. The forehead now feels smooth round to the temples and the scalp feels loose and may tingle.

Tension headaches can be controlled by becoming skilled in relaxing the *frontalis* muscle. Being able to let go from tension in the forehead and scalp will also prove useful as a counter to worry.

Checking: Without tensing them and thinking only of letting go and relaxation, let your attention-awareness dwell again on the muscles of the neck, throat, jaw, lips, tongue, eyeballs, and finally the forehead and scalp. What you are doing (or really not doing) is the awareness procedure you follow in Programme Two. If you spot any tension in any muscle group, let go from it. Keep your eyes steady and at rest and your jaw slack, teeth parted.

The feeling of relaxation in the face is pleasant and you will probably have the sensation that your face has broadened and is now more smooth. You may find it helpful to think of smiling, perhaps even consciously to smile slightly.

Remember this relaxed expansive feeling and adopt it at times when you will benefit most from it. It is incompatible with anger, anxiety or any turbulent emotions; or, for that matter, with narrow rigid attitudes and beliefs.

The mind-calming technique

There are two more groups of muscles that you should learn to relax. These are the imagery and speech muscles that work subtly in the act of thinking. Control over the visual and speech muscles quietens and calms the mind and nervous system.

If the same attitude of attention-awareness that was given to tensing and relaxing hand, thigh, or jaw is brought to the functioning and relaxing of the muscles involved in visualisation and inward speaking, you will start acquiring the ability to fade out these forms of thinking. Body and mind benefit from even a few seconds' silence and stillness. This section of the training programme will prove valuable when later you start practising meditation. Meditation – at any rate of the type which is most conducive to deep relaxation – is all about quieting the mind's thought-chatter and unrest.

Visual: With your eyes still closed, conjure up before your mind's eye a restful scene. Without straining to do so, make the picture as clear as possible. The best way to do this is by recalling some actual place that you associate with relaxation and happy memories. We have an extraordinary capacity for filing away such visual memories, like photographs or, even better, reels of film. Sometimes the projector starts whirring in our inner cinema, without obvious reason, when we are relaxed, perhaps on the edge of sleep or at moments of relaxed reverie. A childhood holiday, perhaps long out of mind, is recalled with great clarity. Sometimes something seen, heard, touched, tasted, or smelt acts as the trigger.

Choose your memory. Bring up the picture. Bring movement into it that you can follow with your eyes: a running child, a speedboat on the sea, a car, an aeroplane crossing the sky, a scudding cloud, or a stick on a fast-flowing stream.

Be aware of the subtle sensation of tension as you visualise your scene for about thirty seconds. Then let go from that faint sensation of tension so that the picture fades out and darkens. The darkening is made easier if you are relaxing in a room that is dimly lit. Sustain the dark, imageless state for about thirty seconds – then visualise and fade out once more.

Speech: Most of our thinking is in the form of subvocal self-talk. Occasionally one sees people moving their lips as they silently think; often they are old people; but most people think in words without other people being aware of it. Sensitive electrical equipment can nevertheless record the normally unseen movements of the speech muscles: lips, tongue, and larynx.

You can yourself, with practice, become aware of the faint tension involved in this inner speech. Start your practice by saying aloud: 'I am bringing peace to my mind.' Be aware of the sensation in your speech muscles. Say it again, more softly. More softly again.

Whisper the words. Say it subvocally. Finally, *think* it: 'I am bringing peace to my mind.' Think the words again, with minimum tension. There is a difference between *saying* something inwardly and *thinking* it in the most subtle way; though even in the latter exercise a very sensitive machine might pick up the use of the vocal machinery. Note the progressive diminution of tension with each repetition of the words 'I am bringing peace to my mind.' Keep your mind free of thoughts and images for up to thirty seconds. It is far from easy to do this for even such a short time without practice at fading out tension. Here again we have a relaxation training exercise which will prove helpful for the practice of meditation.

Repeat the exercise once more, starting by saying, 'I am bringing peace to my mind' and ending by thinking the words in the most subtle way possible. Note well the diminishing sensation, and conclude by fading images and thoughts out of your mind for up to thirty seconds. If you are successful for even a few seconds, you will savour mental stillness and silence that is deeply restful.

Programme Two

The four to six weeks you give to the conditioning controls of Programme One is time well spent; for what you have learned is a technique that could be yours for the rest of your life. What you learn is conscious control of your voluntary muscles. During the final week of daily practice of Programme One you may find it advantageous to produce only small amounts of tension in your body muscles. To be able to let go from faint amounts of muscular tension is a valuable skill to acquire. The modicum of tension may be produced by the methods described in Programme One, but an alternative to those depending on movements – such as raising straight fingers to contract the upper hand or flexing the arm to contract the front upper arm (biceps) – is to use a direct mental command to 'tense!' and then to 'let go!', as you already do in tightening the buttocks. The more you can learn to tense and let go your muscles by this most direct of methods, the greater will be your sense of being in control of your states of tension and relaxation.

You have already learned your relaxation for Programme Two through the training of Programme One. The former differs from the latter in that you no longer deliberately tense muscles. Your attention travels again over your arms, legs, trunk, and face, in what should by now be a familiar sequence of segments – but now you let go from any tension that may be there, without consciously causing it. The amount of tension will most times be small, but you have developed skill in detecting it and in the non-doing which means it is no longer there.

As before, you lie on your back or sit comfortably, in a position conducive to relaxation and in the most favourable available circumstances. Again, you help create the right mood, attitude, and body state for relaxation by stretching like a cat for a few seconds, closing your eyes lightly, and being aware of your breathing for a minute or two. And again, it is attention-awareness, moving like a torch beam from muscle group to muscle group, that acts like a solvent, removing tension.

In Programme One your attention stayed eighteen seconds or so on each muscle group: six seconds of deliberate contraction and twelve seconds of awareness of letting go (relaxation). In Programme Two attention alights on a muscle group and in the first few seconds awareness is established. Any tension there? Start letting go and let the muscles relax for twelve seconds, after which you shift attention-awareness to the next body part in the sequence. *Let go fully* so that tension drains away and the muscles feel limp and the body parts that have contact with bed, couch, floor, or ground feel heavy and sinking down. When you deliberately tensed these parts in Programme One, they will have felt as though they wanted to rise. Warmth in muscles also favours relaxation, so thoughts of heaviness and warmth in your muscles usually help you to relax more quickly and deeply.

Keep attention-awareness active. But otherwise relaxation is passive, a willing and happy surrender to deep rest.

The sequence is as before, and given below for a person whose right hand and right leg predominate. Your whole hand and foot can now be held in awareness as a single unit.

Right hand
Left hand
Right wrist and forearm
Left wrist and forearm
Right upper arm (biceps)

Left upper arm (biceps)
Right upper arm (triceps)
Left upper arm (triceps)
Right foot
Left foot
Right ankle and front lower leg (shin)
Left ankle and front lower leg (shin)
Right rear lower leg (calf)
Left rear lower leg (calf)
Right front upper leg (thigh extensors)
Left front upper leg (thigh extensors)
Right rear upper leg (thigh biceps)
Left rear upper leg (thigh biceps)
Buttocks
Abdomen
Lower back
Upper back
Chest
Shoulders
Neck
Throat
Jaw
Lips
Tongue
Eyes
Forehead and scalp
Visual muscles
Speech muscles

At this juncture it is likely that you will have five or more minutes remaining to complete a relaxation session lasting twenty minutes. A quick look at a watch or clock is permitted, then close your eyes and continue to the twenty-minute mark in one of the following ways:

1   Go over the full programme, devoting five or six seconds this time to each muscle group in the arms, legs, trunk, neck, throat, face and scalp. Conclude again by calming the mind, by relaxing the muscles involved in thinking: imagery and inner speech.

2   Let go with your visual and speech muscles as often as necessary to elicit stretches of mental stillness and silence.

3   Let your attention dwell on the gentle rise and fall of your abdomen as you breathe in and out respectively. By this time your muscle relaxation should be deep and your breathing should be quiet, smooth, and regular.

4   Imagine yourself by the sea, in the country, in a beautiful garden, or otherwise participating in a very restful situation. Though visualisation may be involved, the most important thing is to have the *feeling* of actual participation.

Recall of some actual experience is usually more effective than attempting an imaginative creation, though some people have a special talent for the latter and may prefer to do so. Either way, let as many of your senses participate as possible. If you choose to be by the sea, you should see the waves and sky, hear their encroachment and withdrawal on the beach or shingle, feel the warmth of the sun on your skin, taste the salt in the air and have the smell of seaweed in your nostrils. But if it works best, think of yourself sunbathing with eyes closed.

One or more of these techniques for the final minutes of relaxation probably will be more effective than others, but to avoid any risk of staleness dulling this part of the relaxation programme it should be possible sometimes to vary the method you use.

4

Poised Posture and Body Use

'I hate all knowledge which does not immediately prompt me to action and does not enrich my activity,' Goethe said. Knowledge of relaxation enriches activity, primarily because it is a practical knowledge rooted in body awareness.

The feel of relaxation with which you become familiar through practice of Programmes One and Two can be carried into physical activity. It can contribute to walking and running, to lifting and carrying, to digging in a garden, to washing dishes, to driving a car, to working and to playing. Of course, relaxation in action is of a different kind to the *passive relaxation* experienced as you go through the sequences of Programmes One or Two. Apply passive relaxation to any of the activities named, or even to standing upright, and you would fall in a heap on the floor. *Active relaxation* requires that certain muscles be contracted – those muscles essential for the task – and that muscles not required for efficient performance be relaxed. Dr Edmund Jacobson calls this efficient body use 'differential relaxation'. Some writers on relaxation call it 'dynamic relaxation', though I personally find that too striking a term. Joseph Kennedy calls it 'rhythmical relaxation', though that may place too heavy an emphasis on what is but one aspect of relaxation in action. The word *poise* describes it neatly, both as an experience and as something which at its best can be observed by others. It manifests as balanced posture and as fluent, economical, and effective movement. It is not unrealistic to aim to have it throughout day-to-day activity.

Poised action in specific activities cannot be learned from a book, though helpful guidelines and tips can be given. A description of the muscular interplay in even the simplest act would require thousands of words and advanced knowledge of anatomy, and in the end be of no practical help to the reader. More than one hundred muscle movements are needed to stand up from a sitting position. But helpful guidelines and tips for better posture and more efficient body use can be given: this advice has to be applied in actual experience.

No excess effort

It has already been said that *for poised action only muscles essential for any task should be contracted, other muscles should be relaxed.* A corollary is that *no excessive effort should be made: just the right amount of energy should be applied to any task: no more, no less.* This is worth bearing in mind even in such everyday activities as reading, writing, seeing and speaking. If we apply this principle in both minor and major activities, energy wastage will be checked and rich reserves of energy will accumulate – prompting us to action, as Goethe desired.

Poise – a balance of contraction and relaxation with economy of effort – is exemplified in the great dancer, pianist, or violinist; in the great skier, boxer, or footballer; but also in the expert gardener, motor mechanic, or home help. The principles of poised posture and efficient body use apply to activities of every kind.

The ability to relax well doesn't make an individual master or mistress of every physical activity. In advanced psychomotor skills, the level of success will be influenced by age, sex, physical build, and other factors. Such skills require diligent training based on repetition until the right movements become habitual. But relaxation has an important contribution to make to training for artistic and sporting skills and in giving of one's best in performance.

Checking for unnecessary tensions

As already pointed out, the feel of muscle relaxation experienced in sessions of passive relaxation will provide a sound base for developing skills in differential relaxation. This grounding in body awareness can be supported by checking for unnecessary tensions in the musculature at times during the day. Only a few seconds on each occasion need be given to this act of checking. This is worth doing at any time, but it is advantageous to do it several times daily during the first two or three months of training in relaxation or until you feel that poised action has become habitual.

Contracting muscles not essential to a task squanders energy, creates imbalances in posture and in action, and militates against efficient performance.

Physical activity is carried out by a combination of contracting or shortening muscles and relaxing or lengthening them. One muscle group contracts while its antagonist group lets go and pays out slack. For example, when you bend an arm and firm the biceps muscle at the front of the upper arm, strongman fashion, the triceps muscle at the rear of the upper arm lets go and lengthens. When the triceps contracts, as in pushing a weight to arm's length overhead, the biceps let go and lengthen.

When muscles work in a balanced way in the performance of some task, active relaxation or poise is manifested. Only muscles essential for the specific task are contracted, and then only to the extent required; muscles not essential for the task are relaxed and do not interfere or involve the person in unnecessary effort. There is economy of effort.

Most people have more than enough energy to see them through even a busy day, but many men and women are wilting by late afternoon because they have been frittering away energy in numerous unnecessary muscle tensions and body movements. Gripping the steering wheel tightly does not help a person drive a car; clenching fists or knitting the brow does not help a person think through a problem. It would be easy to give hundreds of examples of energy wastage common in daily life. Most cases of energy wastage are connected with postural faults and poor body use, which go together.

Poor design (from a postural point of view) of chairs, sofas, beds, car seats, and much household, industrial, and office equipment adds to the strain on bodies which more often than not are being held and used poorly in the first place.

Faulty posture

Poor posture is a familiar sight in Western society. It produces muscle tensions, compresses and perhaps twists the spine, cramps body organs, impairs breathing and circulation, strains joints, and causes unnecessary fatigue.

Harmful posture takes many forms, but for illustration we describe two contrasting postural types, which between them encompass the majority of faults commonly seen today. They provide body images in relation to which the look and feel of poised posture may be better gauged. The two incorrect postural types are first, a slumping, slouching, drooping, or sagging posture, and second, a rigid posture of exaggerated erectness, maintained by muscular tension. Slumped posture and rigid posture are frequently seen in Western society. Excellent examples of poised posture are not commonly seen in the West.

The spinal column

The key to postural faults and to postural efficiency is the position and movement of the head, which if it is not poised lightly and centrally will cause the spine to compensate in some exaggeration or distortion of its natural gentle curves.

The vertebral column is the main support of the trunk and protects the spinal cord. It is not straight but S shaped. It is made up of thirty-three irregular bones called vertebrae, each with a disc-shaped body at the front and an arch of bone at the back. We will discuss these from the top down. The seven *cervical* vertebrae are the smallest in the spinal column, with a slightly forward curve. Because the lower vertebrae jut out at the back of the trunk, some people imagine that the cervical vertebrae run down the back of the neck, whereas their location is nearer to the centre of the neck. They support the head, which pivots from a position approximately between the ears. Here again, many people have a wrong image, this time of the head pivoting lower than it actually does, in the neck. These points are worth noting, for they have a bearing on how the head is held and used. The spinous process at the top of each of the cervical vertebrae is forked, which is not found in lower vertebrae, allowing for the passage of a strong ligament which supports the head. The first and second vertebra are the atlas and the axis vertebra respectively. The former is a ring of bone with two sockets on its upper surface which form the joint by which the head nods. The axis vertebra has a projection at the top which passes through the ring of the atlas vertebra, providing the pivot on which the atlas and the head turns.

There are twelve *dorsal* or *thoracic* vertebrae running down the back of the thorax, the part of the body between the neck and abdomen, with a backward curve.

The five *lumbar* (lower back) vertebrae are the largest in the column. They run down the back of the abdomen, making a slight forward curve.

The five *sacral* vertebrae are fused together to form the bone known as the sacrum, running down the back of the pelvis and forming a backward curve.

The four *coccygeal* vertebrae are also fused together to form one bone called the coccyx, which is a tailbone remnant according to evolutionary theory.

Slumped posture
In this posture gravity seems to be inflicting a defeat on the individual; for most body parts slump and sag. But it is the person, not a law or force of gravity, that is responsible for the posture.

The head sinks down between the shoulders and droops forward, like a wilting flower, placing a double strain on the upper spine – both compressing it and pulling it forwards. A chain of postural imbalances and disruptions follow the incorrect placing of the head.

The cervical vertebrae and the dorsal vertebrae are forced outwards, exaggerating their curves and rounding the upper back.

The shoulders come forward and close in, collapsing and flattening the chest. The upper body now presses down on the abdomen, causing it to drop and to protrude. The pelvis is tilted forward and the lower spine and back curved more forward than it should be.

So in slumped posture two common postural defects are found together.

Kyphosis, round back, usually with round shoulders, is the most common postural defect. In most cases the problem has been caused by carrying the considerable weight of the head forward of the vertical axis. The more forward the head, the greater the strain on the muscles of the neck and upper back and on the cervical and dorsal vertebrae. Carrying the head forward can be caused by poor posture for sedentary work, by self-consciousness about being tall,

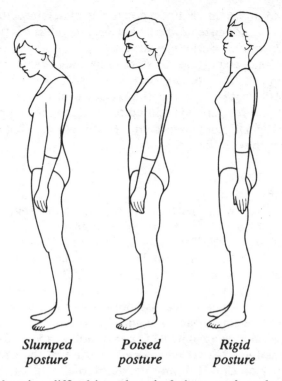

| Slumped posture | Poised posture | Rigid posture |

sight or hearing difficulties, chronic fatigue, and weakness of the neck muscles.

In *lordosis*, or hollow back, the forward curve of the lower back is exaggerated. It is common in very young children, but it does not usually persist. However, in some children it does persist. Some children acquire hollow back as a habit and it may persist into adulthood.

In slumped posture the movements of the thorax and the diaphragm in breathing are restricted, making that function less efficient. The spine is under stress, and there may be harmful pressure on nerves in various places. Strains are imposed on muscles, ligaments, and joints throughout the body. The viscera, the organs the abdomen houses are pressed closer together and may become congested because of impeded circulation. The organs in the narrowed thorax also have less space in which to function. Symptoms often blamed fatalistically on gravity's drag are likely to appear if slumped posture is maintained for years. Women may experience problems because the uterus is tilted forward and down; the ovaries may also sag.

Overall, slumped posture is a state of partial collapse, requiring more energy and effort to maintain than a healthy poised posture. It would be erroneous to connect the slackness of this posture with relaxation: real relaxation is related to poise, not to sloppiness or weakness. Rigid posture, as its name reveals, is more obviously not connected with relaxation.

Rigid posture
This posture is characterised by exaggerated erectness and stiffness. The head is pulled back and down, contracting the neck muscles and compressing the spine. The shoulders are pulled back, squeezing the shoulder blades together and thrusting the chest out and up. The bottom juts and the pelvis is taken too far back.

Strangely, this faulty posture is encouraged in much military training. I say 'strangely' because poise, not rigidity, is the most favourable state for a man or woman who might be called into dynamic action at any moment. Contrast militaristic stiffness with the erect, unforced, alert and poised posture of the Chinese or Japanese person skilled in any of the martial arts. In the latter posture the tonus is just right for swift and decisive action, either in defence or in attack.

It might be thought that, in relation to slumped posture, rigid posture has a redistribution of body parts in the right direction. The head is pulled back and does not droop; the chin is raised and does not sag; the shoulders are pulled back, not dragged forward and down; the chest is raised, not collapsed; the pelvis is pulled back, not tilted forward; the abdomen is pulled in, not protruded; the back is creased, not rounded into a 'widow's hump' . . . The trouble with rigid posture is that its compensations are over-compensations and its corrections are over-corrections. It brings to mind the story of the country parson who prayed loudly before his Sunday congregation for the ending of a period of drought. When rain fell solidly for a week, flattening crops and causing severe flooding, the parson felt called upon to make some pulpit comment on the changed state of the weather. 'Yes, God, I prayed for rain,' he declared. 'But *this*' – gesturing towards the rain-soaked windows – 'is ridiculous!'

Here again there are unnecessary muscle tensions, not this time to prevent the body collapsing, as in slumped posture, but because the body is being forced into sustaining an unnatural erectness. Excessive energy is being employed to support an image of ramrod straightness that does violence to the natural gently curved shape of the spine.

Rigid posture, when sustained for long periods, causes wear and tear on the spine and other body parts. Chronic muscle tension is associated with high blood pressure. In slumped posture it is obvious that breathing is being cramped by the slumping of the chest muscles. In rigid posture it might be thought that the raised, pouter-pigeon chest would encourage effective breathing. It doesn't, because only high chest breathing is encouraged; the full depth of diaphragmatic–abdominal breathing is missed out. The rigidity includes a partial contraction of the breathing muscles. In this and most other respects rigid posture is no improvement on slumped posture.

From a consideration of these two postural extremes, slumped posture and rigid posture, you should already have some conception of what a healthful posture entails. I am calling it poised posture.

Poised posture

This is a healthful posture, whose basic principles apply in standing, in sitting (with obvious differences), and in work and in play. In comparison with slumped posture there is an unforced lengthening and easing up of the body. There is also a natural easy expansion, most noticeably in the shoulders, lower thorax, and across the back. Persons cultivating poised posture for the first time are likely to find an increase in height, in shoulder's width, and in chest circumference. The greater freedom allowed to the breathing muscles in large part accounts for the expansion of the thorax.

In poised posture you do not overcompensate or overcorrect the harmful sag of slumped posture, as you would in rigid posture, but *allow* the body to adopt a lengthened and expanded status. *Think* tall, but don't strain upwards. Here again, the way you carry your head is the primary control or movement. The crown is the highest point of the head. If the analogy helps, think for the moment of your head as a tulip lightly poised on its stalk, or a balloon floating on top of the torso. The neck muscles stay relaxed, and the head, neck, and torso are in alignment. The posture is one of easy, natural balance, from which action can naturally flow.

The body parts are evenly distributed around a central (invisible) line, drawn, as it were, from the centre of the top of the skull to a point between the feet. The feet, pointing straight forward, should be placed about six inches apart and provide a firm platform for even support of body weight. The weight is taken by the whole surface of the feet: the balls of the toes share in the support work, without flexing the toes. The patellae (knee-caps) face forwards, and the knees are extended, but not 'locked'.

The shoulders are not taken forward as in slumped posture or pulled back as in rigid posture, but are kept level with the ears and hanging loosely; raising the shoulders is usually a sign of tension in that area. The shoulders are rotated laterally and held so that the scapulae (shoulder blades) are flat. Let your arms hang by your sides, elbows extended but not 'locked', the palms of your hands against the sides of your thighs, fingers relaxed. The pelvis should be tilted neither forward nor backward.

The thorax is allowed its natural expansion, so that the sub-cortical angle (the bony inverted V on the central line at the front of the body a little below the level of the breasts) is held open.

The breathing muscles – the thorax, the diaphragm, and the abdomen – have freedom to function. So do the vital organs within the thorax and the abdomen.

The torso feels buoyant and does not press down on the abdomen and hips. The hip and the leg joints take the body weight evenly and are not subjected to abnormal pressures. The abdomen feels free and responds easily to breathing rhythms; it has good tone and has not been forced down and out as in slumped posture or back towards the spine as in rigid posture.

Gravity is no longer the problem it was made in the other two postures – surrendered awkwardly to in slumped posture, fought against tensely in rigid posture.

When poised posture is observed full frontal, the body parts should be seen to be distributed harmoniously around a vertical line passing down the middle of the forehead, between the eyebrows,

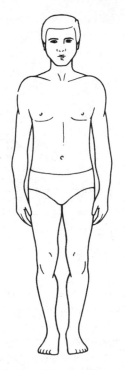

*Poised
posture*

centrally down the nose, the chin, the Adam's apple, the sternum, the sub-cortical angle, the abdomen, the genitals, and reaching the floor evenly between the feet.

Observed from the side, the vertical axis from the middle of the skull would pass straight down by the ear, mid-way through the thorax, abdomen, and thigh, then gradually shift toward the knee and the shin, to finally reach about the middle of the foot.

Note the good alignment and harmonious distribution of body parts, also the absence of strain or tension.

Poised sitting
The instructions given for poised posture standing apply almost in their entirety to poised posture sitting, with the obvious difference in the latter of the flexing of the hip and knee joints.

Again, the crown is the highest point of the head. There is an upward release of the head, torso following. Think tall, think

*Poised
sitting*

expanded, as you sit without strain. Standing or sitting, you allow yourself to come to your full height. Why settle for anything less? *Allow*, not force, yourself to stand or sit at your full height.

An upright chair is most conducive to good sitting posture. The chair seat should be flat and firm and the right height for both feet to be flat on the floor, about six inches apart, and the hip and knee joints having a flexion of about ninety degrees. The thighs should be well-supported and kept parallel to the floor. If the chair has a lower seat and your knees are higher than your hips, extend the knees and the legs a little beyond the right-angled position, but still keeping the feet flat on the floor. If the knees are lower than the hips, the position can lead to tension in the lower back, abdomen, and legs. Sit well back on the seat so that the pelvis and the lower back at least is supported. The instructions already given for alignment of the head, neck, and torso in standing posture apply in sitting posture also. This alignment should be maintained in leaning forward while sitting to eat, work at a table or desk, or to stand up. Remember that the position is one of lengthening and expanding. Keep the shoulder blades flat.

If the position is one of total rest, the hands may be cupped in the lap or rest on the thighs, fingers relaxed.

Crossing the legs, in longer periods or frequent short periods, may twist the lumbar spine and cause aches and pains in the abdomen and lower back which may be experienced without the person understanding that posture has been responsible.

Apply the principles of good posture whatever chair you may have to sit on. To hold good alignment in some chairs, you may have to make use of a cushion placed behind the pelvis and lower back.

Poised walking

This is poised posture moving forward. Think: walk tall – head leading – upward direction. These three instructions are not prior to the movement, but constitute the movement itself. There is no need to lean forward or to thrust your head forward; keep upright without straining upward. Here again you should allow your body to have its full height, the crown the highest point of the head.

If the natural alignment of head, neck, and torso is taken into walking, along with a sense of energy directed upward, walking becomes a floating or gliding movement of surprising ease. Move forward in an even balanced way, without bobbing up and down or rolling from side to side. Relaxed arm movements assist the movement. The shoulders should not be raised. Allow breathing to find appropriate rhythm.

With poised body posture and use, walking becomes the superb exercise it should be, but will not be with wrong posture and body use.

You can 'float' up stairs and down stairs, up steps and down steps, if you continue poised movement with upward direction. You will not need to place your weight heavily on the forward foot before straightening the leg. In descending stairs or steps, the buoyant approach with a sense of energy going upward still applies.

The pleasure and healthfulness of walking will be marred if uncomfortable or unsuitable shoes are worn. High-heeled shoes tilt the pelvis forward and produce an exaggerated hollowing of the lower back and a backward curving or humping of the upper back, thus unnecessarily producing the postural defects of lordosis and kyphosis respectively.

Jogging and running

Walking is poised posture with initiated movement. Jogging is walking speeded up to a trot, and running is jogging speeded up

further. The principles of poised posture still operate. Keep upright; lengthen and expand; release upwards. Think 'energy
directed upward' – you will glide over the ground and go further
with less effort than before.

The Alexander technique

The instructions given so far in this chapter mostly belong to widely
accepted principles of good posture, but some are features of the
system of postural re-education and good body use known as the
Alexander technique. In particular this applies to those instructions
relating to the positioning and use of the head.

Frederick Matthias Alexander was a Tasmanian-born actor and
dramatic recitalist whose theatrical career was threatened when he
sometimes lost his voice. The physicians he consulted were unable
to help. Alexander took to studying his posture in mirrors while
reciting; nine years passed before he hit upon what he believed to be
the cause of his speech problem. He noticed that prior to speaking
he always moved his head backward and down contracting his neck
muscles and compressing his spine. He did the same to start other
actions, and he observed that many other people also had the habit,
though not very young children. Alexander came to believe that the
pattern of head use he saw in himself was a postural fault that
developed for a great many people, and that correcting it would
release tension, free the spine, bring poise to physical activity, and
prove to be useful in the treatment of a variety of ailments linked
with stress.

The Alexander method, which he developed, cured his own
professional problem, but he soon gave up the stage to concentrate
on teaching the method to others. His pupils in London included
George Bernard Shaw and Aldous Huxley. Huxley offered to write
for Alexander, but the offer was refused. Alexander wrote books in
an opaque style that were long on theory and short of practical
instruction. To this day – Alexander died in 1955 – the Alexander
technique has remained an esoteric cult, now classified among the
'alternative therapies'. However, over the years, some highly distinguished men of medicine, science, literature, and the arts have
spoken of the practical benefits and psychophysical value of the
Alexander training. Aldous Huxley stated: 'If you teach an indi-

vidual to be aware of his physical organism and then to use it as it was meant to be used, you can often change his entire attitude to life and cure his neurotic tendencies.' Professor Nikolaas Tinbergen, when awarded the Nobel Prize for Medicine in 1973, devoted half his acceptance speech to describing how he, his wife, and his daughters had benefited from learning the Alexander method of body use. 'There can be no doubt that it often does have profound and beneficial effects,' he said, 'and I repeat once more, both in the mental and somatic sphere.'

Nineteen doctors signed a letter published in the *British Medical Journal* saying they had found the Alexander technique helpful as a therapy and calling for a thorough scientific investigation of its therapeutic use. This has still to be done.

Straightforward, practical accounts of the method in book form were lacking until the 1970s. Sarah Barker's *The Alexander Technique*, a paperback publication of 1978, to some extent does for the Alexander method what Dr Herbert Benson has done for meditation – given us the practical core. The approach to posture and body movement is seen to be good sense, indeed one might say common sense. About the same time that Sarah Barker's book was being published in the United States, Marie Beuzeville Byles' *Stand Straight Without Strain: The Original Exercises of F. Matthias Alexander* appeared in Britain. In it she writes: 'His (Alexander's) technique, mental, physical, and relaxational, is extremely simple and why the practical side has never been written down is hard to understand.' The chief reason, I would suggest, may be found in Alexander's personality and its influence on the people he instructed to become teachers of the method.

The two books mentioned in the preceding paragraph show that if an Alexander teacher is not available or if a person cannot afford or does not wish to pay the considerable fees for instruction, the method can be self-taught from book instruction.

That the aim of the Alexander technique is in accord with our aim of relaxation in action is shown by Sarah Barker's definition of Alexander's key concept of 'use': 'Good use means moving the body with maximum balance and coordination of all parts so that only the effort absolutely needed is expended.'

Head position and use

Alexander came to the view that most postural problems stem from bad alignment of the head with the spinal column. Moreover, crunching the head back and down on the spine perhaps hundreds of times a day leads to the spine becoming strained and misshaped and to wear and tear of the vertebrae. Poor body use, Alexander said, resulted from incorrect positioning and use of the head. Observe very young children, also cats, dogs, and other animals, and you will see that they initiate movements by leading with the head, body following. Persons functioning well do the same. The truth of this we should be able to observe

The alignment of the head with the spine and torso and leading with the head Alexander called the 'primary control'; from it good body use followed, whether it be in lifting a baby, pruning an apple tree, sitting down, standing up, walking, running, speaking, singing, or any other activity.

The primary control is summed up in a verbal formula which is to be thought and used consciously to initiate actions until efficient body use has become habitual. Formulae vary a little in wording according to which Alexander teacher you consult. Alexander's instruction *head forwards and up*, to counteract the tendency to tilt the head backward, is in itself rather misleading, looking more like advice for coping with a tight collar stud or button than with poised posture or movement. *Head forward* means *tilt* forward, not thrusting it forward, which is a postural fault. It should be remembered that the head balances on the top of the spine approximately between the ears, and that the counteracting tilt forward is a nod from what may be thought of as a hinge at the ears and not in the neck as often erroneously conceived. Remember, also, that the *thought* is enough, if it is an aware, experienced thought, to effect the delicate shift in head position that is required.

From a study of various writers on the Alexander technique and experimenting with different formulae, I finally settled for the following:

> *Neck relaxed and free,*
> *Head tilted forward (from the ears),*
> *Head easing up,*
> *Back easing up and widening.*

This formula lets relaxation and poise happen. Its principles can be applied in everything you do. It is essential that the formula should be thought of as part of an integrated action. Sarah Barker, who has taught the Alexander technique at several colleges in the USA, prefers to speak of 'the basic movement' rather than of 'the primary control'. She calls it 'the essence of the Alexander Technique' and describes it as follows: '*As you begin any movement or act, move your whole head upward and away from your whole body, and let your whole body lengthen by following that upward direction.*'

This puts it in a simple and direct way, but a few points need to be made if practice is not to go off the rails.

Upward is a direction and not a place: the direction the top of the spine happens to be pointing. Thus upward is vertical – ceilingward or skyward – when you are standing or sitting upright. But at other times it is diagonal, horizontal, and so on. The direction is horizontal if you have to crawl on your hands and knees into a low tent; it is diagonal before being vertical in rising from sitting in a chair. Complex physical actions may require a stroboscopic pattern photograph to reveal the variety of 'head upward, body following' directions that are taken.

The head has to be thought of as a unit – back, sides, top, and face – and so has the torso, from buttocks to neck.

You should not strain to lengthen the neck and spine, as though in some Lamarckian evolutionary desire to create a race of giraffe-necked people. 'Letting your head move up and letting your body follow', 'allow your whole head to move up and away from your body', 'allow your whole body to follow the upward direction of your head' . . . no straining or striving here.

Letting and *allowing*. Yet there is an *easing up*. Alexander described the movement upwards as 'infinitesimal', Sarah Barker more realistically as 'tiny, in the order of millimetres'. That is why I have been saying that the thought or image is enough to effect the improvement in body use. It *is*, providing that your thought is *aware* and *meaningful* and not casual and mechanical. There is a considerable difference between the two kinds of thoughts, a difference of *attitudes*. A switched-on awareness brings success in learning relaxed action, just as it does in learning passive relaxation.

A useful tip: think, sense, feel, have an image of your life energy directed upward. Again, no striving – the thought, sense, feel, image should be enough to prevent your head crunching down on your top vertebrae and to feel buoyant, as though light-heartedly cocking a snook at gravity and its drag.

The head and torso are joined – so if you ease up with your head, your trunk will follow. Alexander, like a Zen master teaching by paradoxical instruction, used to say: 'All together one after another'. Sarah Barker suggests the helpful analogy of a train: the head is the engine and the torso the linked carriage. I would like to add that the engine driver is a skilled professional, so the movement is smooth at all times, with no jerks or jarring.

To help give their trainees the feeling of poised posture, the spinal column eased up along its linked length, Zen masters suggest taking hold of some hairs on the crown of the head and pulling the head gently upwards. Alexander also taught this exercise to his pupils.

A final point: in the primary movement you should let your shoulders and torso widen as well as lengthen. You should also allow your arms and legs to lengthen.

Schoolchildren and postural education
Alexander pointed out that very young children show good body use. Unfortunately, in Western societies many children soon lose their natural physical equilibrium because they start copying the wrong models, adopt wrong habits of use, sit with poor posture in badly designed chairs, crouch over their schoolbooks, and start losing their muscle sense.

Parents and teachers usually challenge and correct children's bad habits in relation to cleanliness and speech, but bad habits in posture and body use, which can undermine health and impair learning and career ability, are usually allowed to pass without comment because parents and teachers are rarely aware themselves of the harm being done.

Children may acquire postural faults and poor body mechanics through imitating these faults in a parent, teacher, sibling, school-mate, or even a cinema or television idol.

Postural faults may be observed in many five- and six-year olds. If corrections could be started early, these children would have good chances of becoming adults without marked posture problems.

In *Choice of Habit*, published in 1973, Jack Vinten Fenton, an English headmaster with knowledge of the Alexander technique, tells of two six-month projects in postural re-education at a primary school and at a secondary school. Corrections were made to raised shoulders, rounded and hollowed backs, and so on. One primary schoolboy, through postural training, obtained relief from asthma; another from stammering. Release of tension is known to bring relief in both these problems. Improved posture means better body use – which explains why pupils at the secondary school involved in the project started doing better in cookery and in art.

The secondary school pupils built up a collection of newspaper and magazine photographs depicting children and adults standing, sitting, walking, or engaged in some work or play activity; examples of good and poor posture could be studied. The clippings included pictures of people of different races and at different periods in history. This is a useful exercise for any person interested in poised posture. For illustrations of poised posture – women in Africa or India carrying pitchers on their heads, meditating Zen monks or practitioners of Eastern martial arts. For illustrations of faulty posture – look at the photographs in almost any Western newspaper or illustrated magazine.

A more important exercise is to observe good and poor posture and body use in people around you and in yourself.

Posture exercises

Stand erect with your heels two inches from a wall. Without moving your feet, which should be shoulders' width apart, slowly sway your body back until touching the wall. Shoulder blades and buttocks should make contact with the wall simultaneously. If one shoulder blade and/or buttock touches the wall a fraction of a second before the other side, your posture is slightly twisted. If your shoulder blades touch the wall before your buttocks either your upper back has an exaggerated outward curve or you are carrying your pelvis too far forward. If your buttocks make contact with the wall before your shoulder blades, you are carrying your pelvis too far back. If the back of your skull presses hard against the wall, you are retracting your head: the hairs on the back of the head should merely brush the wall.

Now stand with your heels in contact with the base of the wall, and see if your lower back flattens against the wall. If you have an exaggerated forward curve of the lower back or lumbar region, there will be no contact with the wall. This may be achieved by bending the knees forward and flexing the pelvis by lowering the buttocks and tipping the genitals more towards the front. The lower back should be slid down the wall several times.

Another way to flatten the lower back against the wall is to raise both arms straight and forward to a position parallel to the floor. This should be done five times.

Each of these exercises should be concluded by walking away from the wall while retaining the feeling of poised erectness.

The floor may also be used to provide a flat surface for getting the feel of good posture. Lie flat on your back as for the passive relaxation of Programmes One and Two, but flex your knees so that the soles of your feet are flat on the floor shoulders' width apart. Keep your knees up, balancing easily. A rug or folded blanket may be spread for comfort and a slim pillow or cushion placed at the back of your head to keep head, neck, and torso in alignment. Bending the knees means that the lower back flattens and makes contact with the floor, unless there is an exaggerated lumbar curve.

Keeping your back and shoulders flat on the floor, and breathing out through your nostrils, slowly raise your head to a vertical position. Keep your head up, looking at your feet, for five to ten seconds before lowering the back of the head to the floor, breathing in through your nostrils as you do so. Perform five times. This exercise strengthens the neck muscles and aids good carriage of the head. A baby develops the strength to carry the weight of his or her head by repeatedly raising the head from cot or pram and holding it in a vertical position for several seconds.

Each time you lower the back of your head to the floor, think of 'head upwards' and lenghtening and widening your body. This will happen, on a small but significant scale.

You can further aid the lengthening process by making slight and delicate adjustments in your posture. Nod your head slightly a few times without losing the head's contact with the floor and ease your head delicately upwards (i.e. away from your body), and let your body follow, spine lengthening.

Raise your right shoulder and then lower it slowly to the floor, easing it out to the right as you do so. Do the same with your left shoulder. Then right and left shoulder again. Think of the back widening as well as lengthening.

Keeping the soles of your feet firmly on the floor, raise your hips and lower back off the floor. Pause a second or two and then slowly lower the middle back, lower back, and hips to the floor in that order. Feel the lower back settle on the floor. Perform five times.

Return to standing upright by rolling over and pushing yourself up with your hands, leading all the time with your head. You may be surprised how much easier getting up from the floor can become.

Self-observation and checking

Self-observation and alert awareness will help you discover when your posture is out of kilter and when you are about to act from a position that is weak in terms of body mechanics. A full-length mirror will aid self-observation on occasions. Study photographs of yourself; home movies are even better. Is your head being carried too far forward?; too far back?; retracted and crunched down on the spine? Are you tilting your head from the ears or from the neck? Is one shoulder being held higher than the other? Are you bending forward from the waist or back or neck when you could be leaning forward from the hip joints?

If self-observation is objective, a cool appraisal, it will reveal faults of posture and of body use. It will indicate the occasions when energy is being squandered in unnecessary muscle tension and friction. It will show which postural faults have been established and which faulty habits of body use. The discovery of such faults cause the kind of personal shock effect some people experience on hearing their recorded voice for the first time or seeing themselves in a photograph or on film taken from an unfamiliar angle or at an unguarded moment. Most people with poor body use are not aware of the problem. Poor habits of use develop slowly and take over insidiously; they become habitual and are accepted as normal. A trusted friend or member of the family can point out faults, if they have learned what to look for.

Checking is pausing before acting, rapidly appraising your posture and as rapidly making any adjustments that may be necessary. Later, good body use will become habitual and checking will no longer be necessary.

Be aware of your movements, what it is that *you* are doing. When hitherto unconscious actions are brought into the light of conscious awareness, they can be observed and changed if necessary.

Body use

A static image of posture could be detrimental to good body use. Posture, even when motionless, is something that you are *doing*, establishing and maintaining an equilibrium of muscle tension and relaxation. It is important that you have an image of poised posture that is essentially one of relaxed movement.

Efficient, economical body use is not a matter of adopting a series of 'correct' body positions, but of process and movement, of awareness and a sensitive kinaesthetic sense.

The kinaesthetic sense is as important in relaxed action as it is in practising passive relaxation. This important sense is additional to the familiar five. It is sometimes called 'the muscle sense', but it would be more accurate to call it 'the muscle, tendon, and joint sense'. We become aware of it as a sense when we close our eyes yet at the first attempt are able to touch an ear or our nose. Through this sense we judge our position in space and our relationship spatially to objects and other people; it also enables us to gauge the range and the strength of our actions. Without it, we would lack accuracy and coordination in what we do.

The literal meaning of kinaesthetic is 'motion feeling': kinetic, 'motion', aesthetic, 'feeling'. It is this feeling we have for our bodies in action that makes it unnecessary to have detailed knowledge of human anatomy to move efficiently. Through observation and awareness, we can feel what it is we are doing wrong and when we are using our body well.

We develop the kinaesthetic sense as babies and children. In time, other senses, particularly that of sight, tend to overlay the subtle kinaesthetic sense; but if we are aware of its value and its weakening, we can reeducate it.

Practising Programmes One and Two develops a kinaesthetic sense of the difference between muscle contraction and relaxation, whose interplay is seen in all human activities. 'Contrary to some opinions,' writes Jack Vinten Fenton in *Choice of Habit*, 'it is possible to improve movement quality in general by developing sound posture which can be used in any activity'. Earlier in the same book he says: 'Freeing the spine from compression implies dispersing undue and irrelevant muscular tension, since *posture and relaxation are inseparably related*' (my italics). Mr Fenton and other writers on the Alexander Technique think of relaxation particularly in terms of poised action. Relaxation, he says, should be thought of as 'proportionate effort. It is dynamic, not negative. There should be just the right amount of effort for the task – no more, no less. In action this can only be achieved by maintaining good posture.' What I am calling poised posture he calls expanded habit; he likens it to a sponge – 'freed from squeezing it gradually comes to its own shape and bulk, light and open in texture.'

The body cannot function well when its parts are not maintaining a correct equilibrium. That is why learning poised posture is the key to poised action. We should disperse muscle tension that is irrelevant to the execution of any task. At its simplest, poised action refers to relaxing muscles when and where you can and tensing muscles only when and where you have to; this produces a shift to more economical and better coordinated movements.

By cultivating physical poise and relaxed action you can alleviate the pressure of gravity on the human frame at every moment it is in the upright position. The skeleton and musculature receives the greatest strain. The damage done to the body as gravity wins out in old age has been well documented. In the course of the upright waking day men and women lose about half an inch in height; they recover the lost height during the hours of sleep. Old people may become permanently smaller, and some are painfully bent over. Astronauts gain height from a short period of being free from the earth's gravity pull.

There has been a decline in levels of efficiency in body use. This is related to the high incidence of stress ailments and diseases.

Good body use prevents wear and tear, saves unnecessary loss of energy, and improves efficiency in all fields of activity. In general, the body functions with greater freedom and endurance. Muscle tone is enhanced. Muscle tone is not muscle tension, but a kind of alertness, a muscle's readiness for action. The breathing patterns that support action will establish themselves if you use your body well: poised posture, breathing, and action are partners. Having shed tensions that interfered with the action of your breathing muscles, you will find that you are breathing more freely. Improved use of the breathing muscles is likely to produce a broadening of the thorax, which often goes unrecognised until jumpers and waistcoats start feeling tight.

Some systems of physical exercise aid development of the kinaesthetic sense and poised body use. Yoga and slow motion Chinese exercises are excellent in this respect. Yoga exercises are themselves postures rather than repetitive movements. Most dancers are taught good body use. However, if wrong use is brought to the exercises of keep-fit systems, it will impair their effectiveness; physical harm may even be caused, contrary to intention, by vigorous muscular action.

Muscular pattern influences movement: good pattern, good movement, poor pattern, poor movement. If you have been using your body inefficiently for years, then good body use may at first take some time to feel 'right'. Reeducation consists of repeating consciously the correct use of the body until it becomes habitual and feels right and normal. Jack Vinten Fenton tells of eight-year-old David, who had the postural fault of leaning forward. When asked by his teacher to stand up straight, he continued to lean forward, though to his own distorted kinaesthetic sense he *was* standing erect. The teacher then placed the boy in a more vertical position, at which he shouted in alarm: 'Oh, Miss, don't let go! I'm falling backwards!' A new sensory appreciation has to be cultivated for right posture and use to feel right.

Stop, pause, and check
Sensory awareness is the key to dynamic relaxation just as it is to passive relaxation. Pause, observe and be aware of what you are doing with your body and what you are about to do. Frequent checking, frequent initiation of a fresh act with poised body use – that is the way to form healthy new habits. Choose useful moments for checking and practising poised use: for example, at the start of certain acts – sitting down and standing up, going up and going down stairs.

An alert awareness is necessary for acquiring new habits of easy body use, but you should avoid the kind of introspective concentration that causes your movement to freeze instead of to flow. A glassy look in the eyes is a sign of excessive attention; you should be seeing easily and normally at all times. Economical, fluid movement is the aim, so think of flowing movement rather than of fixed positions. Stay 'loose' and 'easy' in the seconds and minutes you give to conscious training in poised use. 'Freezing' of movement is most likely to occur if you practise good use for too long; two or three minutes is enough at one time. Stay fresh and enjoy your practice.

A *choice* of posture and of body habit is possible. Let us see how this works out in some familiar actions and activities.

Leaning forward
A great many adults appear to be ignorant of their own anatomy, to judge by their failures in basic body use. For example, they may lean forward by bending their spines when the best joints to use are those of the hips. As active daily life requires considerable leaning forward, this is one of the most important lessons to learn for economical body use that keeps down wear and tear on the spine.

Think of the torso from pelvis to neck as a unit, and when you lean forward over a desk or table, to work, or to eat, or for any other purpose, to tie a shoelace, to pull up a sock or stocking, to bow in homage, to sit down on a chair or stand up again . . . *make sure you keep head and whole torso in alignment and fold at the hip joints*.

You can get the feel of it by sitting upright on a chair with your feet flat on the floor, a few inches apart, then rocking forward and backward a few times on your sitting bones. Let the movement be effortless and smooth; go forward with head and whole trunk in line and then come back to vertical. Fold at the hip joints and no other part of the body. Stay at ease throughout the exercise; don't contract muscles that do not need to tense. Don't concentrate so hard that your eyes become glassy; they should focus crisply on whatever is in front of you.

Standing up and sitting down
It is a simple matter to continue the leaning forward exercise just described so that you stand up almost effortlessly. Fold forward from the hip joints without altering the relationship between head, neck, and torso. Straighten your legs as the weight of your body comes over your feet. Direct your head and energy upward – diagonal at first, vertical on standing upright – torso following head, lengthening and widening your back. Keep your attention on the

means and suddenly you reach the end: you are standing erect in poised posture.

To sit down, follow the same pattern but in reverse order: fold at the hips, bend knees, lower bottom on to chair seat, sit erect easily. The upward release which helped lift you out of the chair now helps smooth your 'landing'. Strain is taken off your joints and you can lower yourself slowly and easily on to the chair, avoiding the common fault of tensing muscles, as though expecting an electrical shock, and then jolting down. The upward direction of energy should operate both in standing up and in sitting down.

The folding forward movement just described applies to many other activities in daily life besides standing up and sitting down. It reduces friction in body use.

Sitting activities
Basic poised sitting posture was described earlier and is the basis for differential relaxation in sitting activities, such as reading, writing, typing, or driving a car. Remember that head, neck, and torso should be in alignment and eased up, that the head should be lightly poised on the neck, that the shoulders should be kept low and one shoulder not kept higher than the other, that the feet should be a few inches apart with the soles flat on the floor, that the leg and arm muscles should be as relaxed as possible, and that the belly and thorax should move freely, which means unimpeded breathing. Only a modicum of additional muscular contraction will be necessary for most everyday sitting activities.

If you have to lean forward, keep your head, neck, and trunk in line and flex the hip joints, not the back or neck. If you need to turn or tilt your head, always do so from the pivotal point between the ears and not attempt to do so from the neck. Keep your neck muscles relaxed and your head 'floating' high on your neck. Remember, too, that you have muscles which move your eyes in all directions; in some activities the head is frequently turned or tilted forward unnecessarily, as the eye muscles alone could be doing the work.

Reading   Have adequate light coming over your shoulder on to the book, magazine, newspaper, sheet of paper, etc. Support the book etc. with the minimum energy required for efficient reading. Have the reading material at the level and distance that is easiest on the eyes. A bookstand can be helpful in cutting out the muscular effort of holding a book or other reading material and making it easier to view it at an angle which allows for poised alignment of the head and trunk.

Run your attention over your head, torso, arms, and legs and disperse any unnecessary tension. Finally, check that you are not using unnecessary effort in *seeing*; this is easily overlooked. Staring is a form of excessive effort, which hinders rather than aids seeing; it involves muscular tensions and so wastes energy; muscles far removed from the eyes may be tensed. If you think of your gaze as a kind of pressure on the print you are reading, there is one pressure which is most economical and efficient to use: experiment to find it to initiate reading, then allow it to continue. This process is somewhat analogous to focussing crisply an image on the viewing screen of a camera. You have also to keep your awareness switched on for printed words to convey their meaning. If you start switching off awareness you will see how the meaning of the words fades away, even though your eyes are still looking at the print.

Writing Most of the advice given for relaxed reading applies also to relaxed writing. Keep head and trunk in line; flex at hips to lean forward; tilt head at ears, not neck; keep shoulders lightly down, not hunched, at one level, not one shoulder higher than the other; keep neck muscles relaxed, not contracted; keep brow smooth, not knitted; keep eyes relaxed and seeing easily, not staring and straining to see. Grip pen or pencil with just the necessary strength, and press the point on the paper with just the pressure required, no more, no less.

Typing The principles of good sitting posture and body mechanics reduce fatigue and friction for typists. Typists should keep both feet flat on the floor and not tuck one foot behind an ankle or calf; keep head and back in vertical line and forming a right angle with the thighs; keep arms relaxed except for the fingers and hands. The back should be supported. They should stay in poised posture and not stare, which usually happens when tension or fatigue produces it as a compensatory action.

Neck pains
Sitting badly for writing, reading, typing, or any other activity will set up tensions in the neck muscles, and possibly neck pains.

In applying the principles of good body use, remember that the neck muscles should stay relaxed and that this is important for the key head control.

If by checking you discover that you are hunching your shoulders, a frequent contributor to neck pains, then slowly move them up and down a few times. Do consciously what you have been doing unconsciously and note the greater ease when the shoulders are allowed to settle down. Finally, allow them to stay down.

When reading, writing or typing for long periods, it helps ward off fatigue if you occasionally break off for a few seconds and circle your head slowly a few times, clockwise and then anti-clockwise, relaxing your neck muscles as much as possible. Keep your head eased upward. It also helps to yawn and stretch, two of nature's remedies in such situations, or to walk around the room a few times.

Sometimes it is other people that give us a pain in the neck. We may describe such a person as 'a pain in the neck' – but it is *our* neck that is pained, because we contract it. We should either avoid the irritating person, or if we cannot avoid him, then we should try relaxing our neck muscles. Whereupon we may learn to see the better qualities in the person we are reacting to with neck tension. It is interesting to note that we may say of such a person that we 'cannot stand them', or that they 'get up our nose' (which would throw us over backward); these postural metaphors are revealing.

Thinking
This is usually a sitting activity. The practice of Programmes One and Two and the instructions given in this chapter train you to let go from unnecessary tension. This extends even to unnecessary tensions in thinking. When people talk about racking their brains, it is not their brains that are under stress but their muscles, which are tensed hard; this may be happening anywhere in the musculature. We think better for keeping our muscles relaxed.

Help your back

A British expert on slipped discs has stated that 'perfect discs in a modern spine are as rare as perfect teeth in a modern mouth'. In Western countries, back pains are one of the major causes of lost man hours and lost production for industry. Much of this could be prevented by educating workers in good posture and body mechanics.

Every day numerous people are lifting, pushing, pulling, pressing, squeezing, bending, or stretching from positions of leverage that impose severe strains on the spine. Fortunately the spine is a remarkably strong and resilient construction, but it requires all the help you can give it in good muscle tone, sound posture, and efficient body use. In any muscular activity you should aim always for a position of balance and firm support.

For effort with the minimum of strain, the back should be kept comfortably straight and the body parts kept as close as possible around the vertical axis. In reaching down to pick up a load, for example, you should bend your legs rather than arch your back. When the back is kept straight other muscle groups share the work burden. Manual workers learn these things through experience or from older colleagues, but houseworkers, shop assistants, and weekend gardeners may use faulty work techniques for years, causing irreparable wear and tear on the vertebrae and the intervertebral discs.

The arrangement of the spinal column is sometimes described as resembling a swaying stack of children's bricks; hence its resiliency. But it is not designed to take the overloading imposed upon it by weak postural positions.

Lifting

The wrong way to lift a box or other object from the ground is shown in the left-hand diagram (page 92). The main faults with the position are that the feet are too close together, the legs are stiff and straight, and the back is arched. In this posture (which we see all too often) most of the work is being thrown on to the lower back: the chance of a slipped disc or muscle strain is high. Even light objects should not be picked up in this way.

The right way to lift a box or other object from the ground is shown in the right-hand diagram. Note that the feet are spread apart to provide good stability, the legs are flexed to lower the torso, and the back is kept straight. The head is kept in line with the back. In this sitting-on-air position, lifting is achieved by standing up, using the large, strong muscles of the legs and not the small, weak muscles of the lower back. Another factor is that the object is kept close to

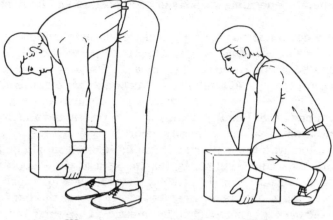

Wrong   *Right*

the body, having been tilted forward just enough for the hands to
get under it. It is lifted with the arms straight.

The same rules apply when the object to be lifted is on a table or
other support below waist height.

Housework

When doing the daily chores about the house backache and spinal
strain will be avoided by following healthy principles of body use.

The wrong way to brush or mop a floor is shown in the left-hand
figure (page 93). The back has been rounded and the feet are close
together. Working for some minutes in this posture will cause backache and fatigue.

In the right-hand figure you see the best posture for brushing or
mopping a floor. The back is straight and head and torso are in
line. The legs have been spread apart and bent at the knees, with
one foot more forward than the other.

Occasionally you may have to go down on one knee or on both
knees to cope with certain tasks: coping with a bottom drawer or
with the bedclothes on a low divan. Thereby you can keep head and
trunk in vertical line.

Squatting on the toes is a position of poor balance. It is useful to
practise squatting down keeping the feet flat on the floor, as people
do easily in many countries of the world, but not in Western
countries. You can squat lower without rising on the toes if you

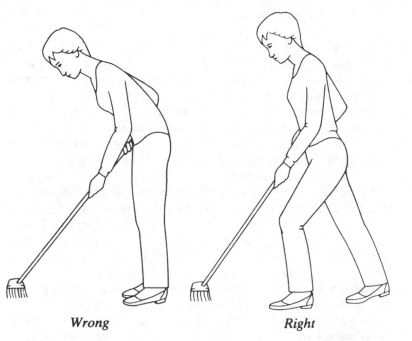

Wrong   *Right*

apply the principle of upward direction, as advised for sitting down.

You may also sit on the floor to work. Here again Orientals are more comfortable in this position than Occidentals. To sit with maximum stability and poise, bend the legs and cross ankles. Keep head and back in vertical line.

Working surfaces Having a working table, desk, or bench at the right height saves the worker from fatigue. Even slight bodily strain causes fatigue, and prolonged fatigue leads to illness.

Try to arrange working surfaces so that you can stay upright to work. Poised posture is the rule again. If you have to lean forward, flex at the hip joints and not at the waist; use a free hand or arm for support when possible.

Pushing or pulling
In pushing or pulling, one leg, bent at the knee, should be forward of the other leg, which may be straight but not 'locked' at the knee. Head, back and straight leg should be in line.

Sport and athletics

Applying the principles of relaxed action will improve performance in any sport, game or athletic event. The so-called 'natural athlete' manifests economy of effort, rhythm, precise timing, relaxation, and poise. The great athlete has learned to relax before powerful effort and even to display a visible measure of relaxation during it, because inappropriate muscle tension is avoided even then. Watch great runners in action and note the relaxed rhythm of their running. In the Japanese film of the Tokyo Olympics I recall close-up shots of the legs of Britain's Anne Packer as she raced to a gold medal, and was struck by the beautiful balance of contraction and relaxation that was clearly visible. Since then I have looked for it in other athletes, seen on television, not only runners, and seen it exemplified frequently by the top performers. In boxing, Mohammad Ali comes instantly to mind: a very big man who, in his own words, could 'dance like a butterfly and sting like a bee'.

Among the clichés of sports journalism are some which point to the factor of relaxation in impressive performance. The best footballers are described as 'making time', 'creating space', 'making the ball do the work', 'staying cool as a cucumber', and 'making it look so easy'. Other sports have similar expressions: 'riding the punch', 'following through', and so on. Economy of effort and physical poise are major features of sports or athletic performances that give aesthetic delight to the spectator.

The principles of good body use or active relaxation described in this chapter are exemplified in the golfer's swing when it is most graceful and effective: feet apart, slight lean forward from the hips, back straight, head in line with trunk, shoulders flexible. Golfers should try the Alexander principle of easing upwards. From poised posture flows a coordinated drive, rhythmical and well-timed, the speed of the descending club head and the rhythmical participation of the whole body producing the distance of the shot rather than brute force. Similar principles apply to punching ability in boxing, kicking ability in soccer, and so on.

If a golfer 'checks' (for tension), he or she should look first at the most obvious sites of harmful tension – in the arms, the shoulders, the hands – but also looking elsewhere because unnecessary muscular tension anywhere is likely to be detrimental to physical skill. A golfer's knees may be too tense. The right leg (of a right-handed player) may straighten on the backswing, but it should not 'lock' at the knee or feel tense. Both knee joints should stay relaxed. So should the wrist joints, which should have 'well oiled' flexibility.

If when addressing the ball a golfer feels that the knees or the wrists feel tense, or both, he or she should step back, walk around a bit, flexing the knees lightly and/or waggling the hands loosely like empty gloves for a few seconds before again preparing to make the shot. One tip I read for unlocking the wrist muscles is to imagine that the ball is just a dandelion top you are about to clip.

These points about playing golf have been taken from a collection of newspaper and magazine clippings I gathered relating to the important part relaxation plays in sport, athletics, games, and the performing arts.

The performing arts

Men and women who give performances of any kind before a gathering of watching people know how muscle tension can be harmful. Physical execution in the performing arts is often precise and delicate and vulnerable to excess effort and tension.

Skilled dancers demonstrate the grace and beauty of dynamic relaxation. So do many of the finest actors and actresses, pianists, violinists, and other instrumentalists. It is true to say that the better the player the more poise in action one usually finds. And, as with sport and athletics, relaxation is a key element both in training for the skill and in public performance.

The celebrated Chilean pianist Claudio Arrau says he learned an important lesson about piano playing when as a student in Berlin he attended a piano recital given by a famous woman pianist. With male pianists, you do not normally see them play in public concerts with their arms bared; but women pianists may wear sleeveless dresses. What Claudio Arrau learned that evening in Berlin was that the hands could supply all the power or delicacy needed in piano playing, yet *the arms could stay relaxed*.

Heinrich Neuhaus, himself a famous pianist and teacher of Emil Gilels, Sviatoslav Richter, and other *virtuosi* at the Moscow Conservatoire, relates in *The Art of Piano Playing*: 'If a pupil did not have full control over his body, in other words when a pupil did not have sufficient freedom, I suggested the following exercises away from the piano: stand, letting one arm drop "lifelessly" like a dead weight alongside the body; let the other "active" hand pick it up by the fingertips gradually raising it as high as possible and having reached the highest point suddenly let go so that it should drop just *come corpo morto cadde* (as a dead body falls).

'Would you believe it? This simplest of all exercises was at first beyond the possibilities of many of the frightened and cramped brigade. They just could not manage to disconnect completely the muscles of the arm which was to be the "dead body". It would come down half way but did not drop (probably because the other hand at the time was very active and thus influenced the first "contagiously").'

The controversial Ivo Pogerelich claims to use a way of holding his hands on the keyboard that gives maximum relaxation and freedom and which was used, according to his teacher-wife, by Liszt.

Herbert Whone, a painter as well as a violinist, wrote in *The Simplicity of Playing the Violin* that the first essential for good violin playing is 'release of all tensions and blockages to freedom in the limbs'. In discussing the alertness needed for good 'attack' – 'animal attack' he calls it – Herbert Whone says the violinist should think of the relaxation of the cat and the 'super-charged stillness' of the moment before it pounces on its prey. He recommends low diaphragmatic breathing and the sense of being firmly centred in the area just below the navel – a Zen concept and practice.

'Contraction is a violinist's chief enemy', he writes. 'It is, as the word suggests, contra-action, against action, and to realise this is the key to control in the body'. Of course, contraction is a relative term; a certain minimal tension is needed for the violinist to hold his or her arms up. One way to achieve the right degree of relaxation or poise is to drop down to it from an exaggerated degree of contraction. The muscles of the raised arm, which is in a position for playing, are tightened to the point of rigidity, then the contraction is gradually released until the arm feels light and free to move easily. This should be done several times with each arm.

For the tension range between rigid immobility and freedom of movement and lightness through relaxation, Mr Whone suggests images drawn from density in the natural world. Maximum contraction is imaged as steel and minimal contraction as air. Between these poles the densities are imaged in descending order as stone, soil, wood, water, and paper. 'By becoming familiar with such states at the shoulder, elbows and wrists, it is possible to control and ultimately transform them at will into the air state. The air state is our objective . . .'. The objective is the state of minimal tension.

This use of imagery for gradations of experienced tension-relaxation may be employed in approaching minimal relaxation in activities other than playing the violin. You may wish to invent your own analogical terms. Photographers could use the photographic grey scale developed by Ansel Adams, which involves visualisation of ten gradations from dense black to pure white to be controlled through exposure and development times. Artists may prefer a colour scale, musicians the tonic sol-fa, and so on.

Relaxation, poised posture and body use are essential factors in good voice production; without them speech or song is constricted, tonally hard, and fatiguing. How could they not be of prime importance in speech and song when the body is itself the instrument? It need not surprise us, therefore, to find that relaxation and posture feature prominently in the training of actors, actresses, and singers. The famous Russian theatre director Constantin Stanislavski valued relaxation exercises highly for dramatic performers. The contribution of poised posture and relaxed body use to ease and beauty of tone has long been appreciated in the training of singers, especially for grand opera, in which carrying power and great vocal stamina are necessary.

Strained speech is not only detrimental to careers in some of the performing arts – it is a cause of tension and fatigue for numerous men and women with no ambitions for the stage or concert platform. There is also the psychologically distressing speech dysfunction of stammering, which is caused by various forms of psychophysical tension.

Physical and mental poise

Oriental poise
It would be an oversimplification to say that certain personality traits automatically accompany certain postures, but there is a

tendency for them to go together. (Consider for a moment how the physical act of smiling encourages a more cheerful mood.) Because of this association, and the connection between posture and health, poised posture has a prominent place in the practices of the Eastern meditative systems, which recognise that 'outer influences inner and inner influences outer'.

The feeling of poise and stability achieved by those who have mastered the cross-legged postures of Buddhism, Yoga, etc. comes in large measure from the alignment of the head, neck, and torso that naturally occurs in these traditional sitting positions. The head is the apex of an isosceles triangle in which the crossed-legs and the buttocks form the base.

One of the two main schools of Zen, the Soto school, is based almost entirely on the practice of poised sitting. And poised posture and body use is an integral part of such Zen-influenced Japanese arts and crafts as calligraphy, ink painting, pottery, flower arrangements, and the tea ceremony, as well as being key elements in the practice of such sports as archery, aikido, judo, kendo (swordmanship) and sumo wrestling. In all these interests, Zen mental poise – attitudes of mindfulness, clear awareness, equanimity, and so on – are close companions of physical poise. In the Zen approach, arts, crafts and sports are systems of spiritual training or 'ways'. Calligraphy, an ink painting, the visible shape of a pot, an arrangement of flowers in a vase, the manner of preparing, serving, and drinking bowls of tea are admired not so much in and for themselves as for what they convey to the discerning viewer about the state of consciousness of the calligrapher, the painter, the potter, the archer, and so on. There is here a philosophy of relaxation and a way of poise.

In Zen, the belly just below the navel is 'the body-mind's vital centre'. But all the requirements of Alexander's 'upward release' are present also. Some of Alexander's exercises are identical with instructions given by Zen teachers. For example, to think of yourself as a puppet being pulled up by a string attached to your topmost head hairs, a Zen instruction, is matched by Alexander's recommendation to grip the hairs on the crown of your head and pull gently upward to encourage the upward release.

The most important thing in Japanese archery is for egotism to be dropped so that 'it is something, not yourself, which draws the bow' and the arrow shoots by itself. Professor Eugen Herrigel spent several years learning archery in Japan and wrote a short, lucid account of his experiences that has become a modern classic on Zen training. Kenzo Awa, the archery master, taught Herrigel poised posture and how to 'pull with the mind' while keeping the arm muscles relaxed. The master had a powerful bow that only he could pull; when he did, Herrigel observed, his arm muscles stayed soft and relaxed.

This Zen approach to sports has been echoed in some books on playing tennis and golf published in the United States.

Dynamic poise

The Japanese view of good posture is upward, yet firm and collected, centred just below the navel, in the belly (*hara*). This posture is symbolically called *ten–chi*, or 'sky–earth'. (For a more detailed account of Oriental concepts of posture see my book *Relaxation East and West*.)

The Oriental understanding is that just as training in emotional and mental poise, such as meditation, promotes physical poise, so training in physical poise brings rewards in increased emotional and mental poise. The link between emotions and breathing rhythms is easily recognised; less obvious is the connection between emotional states and posture, but it is there.

Everyday poise
Poised posture and poised body use are the foundation of efficient, effective and long-lasting active life. However, we should choose to engage in those activities which are consonant with our natural abilities, age, sex, physical build and personality; to go against any of these factors would create friction and tension. The higher skills require diligent training. A wide range of rewarding activities remain for almost every person.

The contribution that active relaxation makes to living is not least in the enjoyment it can bring to 'ordinary' everyday activities. As Dr Eustace Chesser wrote in *Life Is For Living (So Relax and Enjoy It)*:

'The joy of using our limbs has been lost because we use them so badly. When that is recovered a new quality is added to our lives. Instead of seeking artificial pleasures we discover a natural pleasure in the small, inevitable activities that are part of our everyday routine.'

5

Rapid Muscular Relaxation

The full benefits from a programme of neuromuscular relaxation will be obtained by moving your attention unhurriedly from one body part to another in a logical and effective sequence so that the most important muscles in the arms, legs, trunk, and face have let go from tension. Ideally, for deep relaxation, you should devote ten to twenty minutes to it, with best results most likely to come from the full twenty minutes. However, there may be times – *will* be times – when you wish to relax for only a few minutes. Once you have acquired skill in muscle relaxation, having practised daily for several weeks the training and conditioning exercises of Programme One and then become familiar with the more direct approach of Programme Two, you should find even one to five minutes relaxation of the voluntary muscles a refreshing experience.

There are several approaches you can make to short-duration relaxation, and if you have done your homework and trained to let go from tension, you can hardly go wrong with any of them.

Lie on your back or sit comfortably in the best relaxation posture. Close your eyes. Then:

1   Let your attention-awareness, with no suggestion of haste, move steadily up your right (or left) arm from hand to shoulder, removing tension the way a tape recording is erased when you want to record something different. The something different in this case is relaxation. Then relax your left (or right) arm from hand to shoulder. Follow by relaxing your right (or left) leg, then left (or right) leg, from foot to hip. Then move up your trunk, letting go from tension

in your buttocks, abdomen, lower back, upper back, chest, and shoulders. Relax your neck, throat, jaw, lips, tongue, eyes, forehead and scalp. Finally, for the remaining time, relax your visual and speech muscles, producing mental calm.

2   Take slow, deep, quiet, and even breaths, preferably through your nostrils. Become aware of the gentle movement of your lower ribs and abdomen, both of which expand a little on breathing in and subside on breathing out.

Having 'latched on to' the muscular sensations and rhythm of your breathing, without interfering with them, think of tension, strain, and stress flowing out of your body and mind on each release of air from your lungs. Summon all your powers of attention and imagination for this procedure. Feel all your muscles going limp and resting heavily in those places where muscles are supported.

Continue in the above way for the number of minutes available for relaxation.

3   If muscles are deliberately contracted and muscular tension is made the focus of your attention, and then you let go abruptly from that tension, the contrast between the successive states of tension and relaxation enhances the experience of the latter. Some researchers believe that there may be some kind of natural rebound effect, muscles going that little bit further in relaxation than they would have if the muscles had not first been contracted. This suggests a technique for rapid relaxation by shortening the time given to contracting muscles. It should be understood that this shortened version only becomes a useful substitute for the full version (Programme One) when first you have been conditioned by the full training programme.

Become aware of your breathing. On each of three successive exhalations, think of tension flowing out of body and mind.

Now straighten the fingers of your right hand (or left hand) and also straighten the whole arm. Raise the extended arm about two inches above whatever was supporting it, which will be your thigh if you are sitting. Now strongly tense the whole arm from hand to shoulder. After a contraction lasting six seconds, end it abruptly and let the arm flop on to the bed, couch, floor, or ground if you are lying on your back and on to the top of your thigh if you are sitting. For the duration of three in–out breaths, think of the arm becoming limp and resting heavily. In a similar way, contract and relax the left (or right) arm.

Next point the toes of your right (or left) foot and straighten the leg. Raise the heel of the extended leg about two inches above its support. Contract it strongly and be fully aware of the sensation along the leg for six seconds. Abruptly let go, so that the leg flops down to its starting position. Be aware of deepening relaxation in the leg during three in–out breaths. Similarly, contract and relax your left (or right) leg.

Switch your attention to your trunk muscles. By mental direction, contract all your main muscles from pelvis to neck. This means flattening and firming the abdominal wall, squeezing in your chest muscles while at the same time drawing your shoulder blades together, contracting the upper back. Tension should also be thrown into the lower back muscles. Hold the contraction for six seconds, then let go and let your trunk muscles expand and relax for three breaths.

Tense your neck muscles by thinking of lowering your chin on to your chest but preventing any movement by contracting the muscles at the back of your neck. Contract the neck for six seconds, then let go for three breaths.

Finally, contract the facial muscles and let go. Bring eyebrows and cheeks together; press teeth and lips together, contracting jaw and mouth; press your tongue against the roof of your mouth. After six seconds, abruptly let go from tension. Feel your face relax, a sensation of broadening and becoming smoother. Let teeth and lips part slightly. Let your eyelids be lightly down. Think of smiling and of the stillness and serenity seen on the face of the sitting Buddha as depicted in art and sculpture. Hold in awareness the feeling of relaxation in the facial muscles for the remaining time available to you.

6

Relax and Sleep Well

'Come sleep! O sleep, the certain knot of peace,
The baiting place of wit, the balm of woe,
The poor man's wealth, the prisoner's release,
Th' indifferent judge between the high and low.'
                              Sir Philip Sidney

Millions of people call and it does not come. When it is valued so
highly and it doesn't come, it is difficult to resist striving for it; but
trying to sleep keeps it farther away. As restless hours crawl by, the
insomniac could join Shakespeare's Henry IV in protesting:

'O sleep, O gentle sleep,
Nature's soft nurse, how have I frightened thee,
That thou no more wilt weigh my eyelids down,
And steep my senses in forgetfulness?'

In any large anthology of quotations, those relating to sleep are
usually numerous. Sleep is praised by poets and writers, as in the
above lines by Sir Philip Sidney, for the deep rest it gives, its
refreshment, the escape from cares, the way it is available to rich
and poor alike. But the poets write about it also because of the
element of mystery attached to it. Why do we need it? Why does
Nature seemingly intend us to spend about a third of our lives with
consciousness switched off? Scientists have studied the physiology
of sleep and some have produced theories about the origin and

functions of sleep. But sleep remains mysterious, even to the scientist.

Poets have noted similarities between the forgetfulness of sleep and death:

'Care-charming Sleep, thou easer of all woes.
Brother of Death.'

Francis Beaumont and John Fletcher were not the only writers to see a resemblance between the unconsciousness of sleep and that of death. But I would suggest a happier connection: *sleep, brother of relaxation*.

Relaxation and sleep

It is important to realise that relaxation and sleep are two different states of rest – and that we need them both! Both, it is true, are hypometabolic states when reaching their deepest levels. Hypometabolism is a state of decreased metabolism. But whereas during the relaxation response oxygen consumption falls rapidly, with decreases between ten and twenty per cent occurring in a few minutes, the rate of decrease during sleep is gradual and is about eight per cent lower than that during wakefulness after about five hours.

There are other physiological differences between sleep and deep relaxation. For example, electrical activity in the brain shows different EEC patterns in sleep and in relaxation. Alpha waves are more frequent and intense in relaxation than in sleep; during sleep, though some brain cells take rest, others appear to be very active. There is nothing comparable during the relaxation response to the stages observed in sleep.

The EEC (electroencephalogram) records some interesting changes in brain wave patterns during the hours of sleep. The first stage is non-dreaming sleep in which the brain waves are slow. During the second stage agitated movements are recorded on the EEG and the eyes move rapidly behind the closed lids. This is the REM (rapid eye movement) phase in which the sleeper is dreaming. If wakened during this stage, ninety per cent of the people the sleep researchers are studying can describe their dreams clearly. But wakened five minutes after the dreaming stage has ended and only one per cent of the subjects recall anything at all of their dreams. In the third stage, sleep lightens before deepening again. Normally the pattern described happens four times each night, with the dreaming period becoming longer.

According to the sleep researchers, during non-dreaming sleep we replenish our energies and the body engages in repair and growth. Protein production rises – proteins are the building blocks of the body system. If we have taken more physical exercise than usual during the day, or if we have suffered an injury, we spend more time in non-dreaming sleep. Powerful forces work on our behalf.

Dreaming sleep takes up, on average, about twenty-five per cent of total sleeping time. Why do we need to dream? The scientists are less sure about that than they are about the need for non-dreaming sleep. Recent studies point to the dreaming period as an opportunity the brain takes to sort out, re-classify, and generally assimilate the immense mass of information it has been taking in during the active day. What is happening is comparable to clearing and revising a computer program. Scientists who hold this theory point to the fact that young people, who are heavily engaged in the learning process, dream more than adults – and that adults who have themselves become students increase the time spent in dreaming sleep.

Deprived of either non-dreaming or dreaming sleep, we catch up in that department as soon as we can. If we go short of all sleep, the non-dreaming sleep has first claim, then dreaming sleep makes good its loss.

As there is work to be done during sleep, the body needs a certain level of energy at the time of going to sleep. When our body is over-fatigued, sleep will not come until we have relaxed a while and recovered adequate energy levels.

We need relaxation and we need sleep. As we spend about one third of our lives in sleep, it is sound sense to make sure that it is of good quality. The most important thing to remember in this matter is that sleep is of good quality when it is *relaxed sleep*.

Nervous tension (so called) is the chief cause of failing to get sleep, of broken sleep, and of sleep lacking the refreshment it should provide. The more anxious we become about getting to sleep, the more it eludes us; but if we relax and divert our attention away from sleep – then it comes, though we do not know the moment of its coming. The next thing we know is morning daylight, and a new day is about to start for us.

Taking sleeping pills is an unsatisfactory way to obtain sleep, unless in extreme circumstances. In Britain the nightly consumption of sleeping pills is two million. They are addictive, and the sleep they force on the body is inferior to natural sleep.

The ability to relax well speeds the onset of sleep and deepens it. Many people who practise relaxation/meditation daily find they need up to an hour's less sleep than before, but this is not always so. What is usually the case is that these people have greatly increased chances of going to bed without feeling uncomfortably tired, of sleeping well, and of waking refreshed after a night's sleep.

How much sleep do we need?

There have been various theories about the origins of the sleep habit. One of the most recent is the immobilisation theory, in which Dr Ray Meddis, a British scientist and psychologist, puts forward the idea that sleep began as a protective device, a way of keeping animals quiet at a time when activity would be dangerous. He points to the sleep habits of animals to support this theory. Baboons have the nearest sleep patterns to what our primitive ancestors must have had: going to sleep when the sun sets, wakening at sunrise.

Do we still need sleep now that we live lives of comparative safety? Probably not, says Dr Meddis, but millions of years of human evolution have programmed the human brain to sleep.

Perhaps one day scientists will find a way for humankind to do without sleep, or with much less sleep. If that happens, when will the human body work at repair of wear and tear and growth, and the brain computer do its reprogramming? Until these revolutionary changes in human behaviour come about we must make do with seven or eight hours' sleep in twenty-four hours, which is the average requirement for adults. Newborn babies start out with about sixteen hours a day, children of ten need about ten hours, and adolescents about nine hours.

There are some adults who seem to need less than the statistical average. Sir Winston Churchill was famous for only sleeping four hours at night – but he took 'cat naps' during the day. Occasionally one hears of a person who claims to need no sleep at all; invariably, on investigation they are found to doze intermittently for short periods without being aware of it. But the very low sleep need of such people is strange.

Old people often sleep only five or six hours in bed, but usually take naps sitting in a chair during the day.

If we are not having enough sleep, the body lets us know through tiredness and reduced motor and mental efficiency. And when given the chance – at weekends perhaps – the body takes extra sleep and restores the balance.

Slowing down or unwinding

Too much excitement, and in particular an overactive mind, is detrimental to easing into sleep. Ideally, for anyone with a sleep problem, relaxation should start several hours before going to bed. Unwinding is helped by a regular late evening pre-sleep ritual which can be performed slowly and given quiet attention. What it consists of depends on individual interests: reading poetry or a novel, listening to music on radio or record, watering house plants, setting a table ready for breakfast – each person finds his or her own ritual.

We find through experience what our body tolerates in the few hours before sleep, and what over-stimulates. What affects one person does not necessarily affect another person. A late drink of coffee or tea may keep one person awake, but not another. Generally, late meals and over-indulgence in alcohol or tobacco do not favour sound sleep.

The solution to over-stimulation is the same as that to over-fatigue or over-tiredness: to be patient and relax, waiting for the body to be ready for sleep. Anxiety only creates further stimulation.

In most circumstances, the techniques for relaxation learned from this book will prevent the kind of build-up of tension in muscles and mind that is inimicable to sleep.

Conditions conducive to sleeping

The instructions given for preparing to relax lying on your back also apply to preparing for sleep: empty bladder, quiet, dark or dimly lit room, and so on. For relaxation you may or may not lie on a bed;

nearly everyone does so for sleeping. The mattress should be firm, but not so firm that it is uncomfortable to lie on. A soft mattress causes parts of the body to sink lower into the mattress than other parts. One pillow – perhaps two thin pillows – will keep the head in alignment with the torso. This factor in poised posture should be observed in sleeping as in activity.

It is customary to reduce sense stimuli when wanting to sleep. Darkness or semi-darkness reduces stimulation of the sense of sight, and the eyelids are lowered, echoing the lowering of window blinds. Loud noises prevent sleep, but most people can tolerate a certain amount of noise if the sounds are familiar. People who live beside a railway line become used to the noise of passing trains, but visitors who stay some days are kept awake by the trains, at least for the first night or two. Unfamiliar repetitive noises, trivial in themselves, can prove irritating. The ticking of a clock always in the bedroom gives no trouble, but a dripping tap or creaking window may prevent sleep until the problem has been attended to.

The sense of sight is the first to fade as we drift into sleep, and the sense of hearing goes next. The sense of touch is the last to relax, though it does not entirely go off duty; it stays sensitive to changes in temperature, and we unconsciously pull up the covers if they slip down the bed.

Letting go for sleep

We say that we 'fall asleep'. The word 'fall' implies *letting go*. There is nothing fearful about this fall: most people welcome it, for there is a safe, soft landing.

The mind or brain is the key controller in falling asleep. Letting go mentally is the major factor in slipping into sleep; but the mind cannot let go when the messages the brain receives from the body muscles is of tension or when the emotions are heaving or thoughts are on the boil.

Some people go to sleep almost immediately on their heads touching the pillow, whereas others like to indulge for a few minutes in a gentle reverie, with wisps of images drifting before the mind's eye and some inconsequential thoughts flashing momentarily, before passing into sleep.

Worry and tensions of any kind prevent sleep coming and are

likely to disrupt it after it has come. An overactive brain needs to slow down before sleep hears its call; techniques for doing this have been described in earlier chapters.

There is a Zen story about two monks who while on a long journey on foot come to a stream that has to be waded across. Gallantly, one monk carries a young woman across on his back. The two monks walk on together in silence for two hours before one speaks uneasily, querying the propriety of the other monk in having contact with the young woman's body. Back came the reply: '*I* left the young woman back at the stream. I perceive that *you* are still carrying her.'

To relax the mind and prepare it for sleep, we need to put the day's events behind us, as the Zen monk had done with a happening two hours earlier. Sometimes the events are too powerful, but awareness of the problem and practice can achieve much in this direction.

On going to bed, it will help bring sleep closer to lie in the position on the back for passive relaxation and allow the beam of attention to play over body parts in sequence from feet to face, concluding with relaxation of the eyes and vocal muscles. This is, of course, the practice of Programme Two.

Focus attention on each body part for about ten seconds. This will give sufficient time for awareness to dissolve tension in the muscle or muscle group. Move easily and without urgency through the letting-go sequence. When all the body parts have received the focus of attention, you then have a choice of several ways of continuing relaxation. Sleep may supervene at any point – but not if you keep looking for it! Where your attention rests at any moment in a sequence is the right place to be.

Having moved your attention from your feet to your face, letting go from tension, you could again travel over the course in awareness, first thinking of the muscles becoming heavier, then suggesting to yourself that the muscles are becoming warmer. Feelings of heaviness and warmth are conducive to deepening relaxation. The therapy of autogenic training uses suggested heaviness and warmth in a few body parts. A key area to focus on in autogenic training is the solar plexus, an important network of nerves behind the stomach. The suggestion is given 'solar plexus becoming warm and glowing'. If you relax from feet to head for the third time, suggesting increasing warmth, then the solar plexus could be included. We know how the stomach is felt to churn when we are nervous, so this area could be important to promote relaxation and sleep. It may help to imagine warm sunlight shining on the area, or a hot water bottle resting on the stomach.

Self-talk for feeling the body becoming heavier may be worded on the lines of 'my feet feel heavy as lead; they hold my heels firmly on the bed', and so on. As you go over the body from feet to face in this way, pause occasionally and be aware of the pressure of the bed against your heels, calves, backs of thighs, buttocks, lower and upper back, shoulders, neck, and back of head. The pressure should be evenly distributed between right and left sides of the spinal column. Feel that, for some minutes at least, there will be no possibility of moving.

The three awareness programmes are – first, letting go from tension in the muscles; second, muscles feeling heavy; third, muscles feeling warmer. You are likely to go to sleep at any time.

Another relaxation technique that may be used is some form of visualisation. A favourite scene that elicits feelings of relaxation may be visualised. Other senses may cooperate in the illusion: listening to the sound of waves breaking on a beach or of the sea sucking at shingle, of a purling stream, the vocal ecstasy of a lark, and so on. If sensory evocation does not come easily to you, concentrate on some of the other relaxation methods.

You may use one of the meditation practices described in Chapter 7. Awareness of breathing is particularly suitable. The gentle rise and fall of the abdominal muscles in diaphragmatic–abdominal breathing is conducive to easing one's way into sleep.

An appropriate *mantra*, such as 'let go' or 'peace', may be repeated mentally on exhalations, or breathing awareness by itself used to bring a pleasant glow of comfort. When the body is comfortable and relaxed, it is ready for sleeping.

Sleeping position

If you prefer to lie on your back for going to sleep, then keep relaxing, bodily and mentally, until sleep comes. But sleeping on one's back encourages mouth breathing and snoring. Most authorities on sleep say that lying on either one's left or right side is the best sleeping position. We instinctively change positions during the hours of sleep, thus preventing muscular aches and sores, but each person has a favourite starting position which is the one they most often return to.

The heart is protected by the thoracic cage, so it does not matter whether we sleep on our left side or on our right side.

The following position is thought to give maximum comfort and support for the body, with a minimum of pressures on the respiratory muscles and internal organs. It will be described here for lying on the left side, but the instructions may be adapted easily for the right side. Lie on your left side, and gently flex your left arm so that your left hand rests on your right shoulder. Your right arm should also be bent at the elbow and be supported by the mattress or partly by the mattress and partly by the abdomen. The right leg, flexed at the knee, rests a little in front of the left leg. The left leg may be extended without being 'locked' at the knee. In this position the shoulders can be kept wide apart and not squeezed in on the chest so as to restrict the breathing muscles. The pillow may be pulled into the angle between neck and shoulder if it favours good alignment of head and trunk.

Having too many pillows places a strain on the neck muscles and on the cervical vertebrae. A similar strain is imposed by lying on the belly and twisting the head to one side; this can be responsible for neck pains, headaches, and cervical lesions.

There may be medical reasons why the preceding on-side position cannot be strictly adhered to. For example, sufferers from asthma may need to prop up the head and trunk in a higher position than the pelvis and legs.

Other on-side positions than that recommended above may be adopted for a few minutes at a time without our coming to any harm. For example, one leg may rest on the other for a few minutes and the hand of the uppermost arm allowed to rest on the uppermost thigh.

When you lie in the passive relaxation position and use your directed attention to relax your muscles and to quieten your mind, a point should come when you feel ready to turn slowly and gently on to your favourite side and to let go further. If sleep supervenes while you are still lying on your back, it is almost certain that soon you will turn involuntarily in your sleep. Otherwise the time to turn on to your side is when you feel comfortably and warmly relaxed and there is a pleasant melting and merging of sensations.

Other methods

There are other methods of attracting sleep which may work for some readers, or which they may wish to keep in reserve, as it were.

One of these is to take slow, progressively shallower diaphragmatic–abdominal breaths. There are physiological reasons for this approach. The method is most likely to work if you precede it with some minutes of muscular and mental relaxation. Of course, it may not then be necessary. Using this method for some minutes, it would be natural for one or two large oxygen-recovery breaths to occur involuntarily.

Visualising pleasant scenes has already been mentioned. Another visual technique is to picture a grey screen filling the whole of your visual field. At the centre of the grey screen visualise a small black dot. The technique is to very gradually expand the black dot until *it* fills the whole of the visual field. Blackness will then have replaced greyness. See total blackness, which is restful for the eyes, for four or five minutes. Then repeat the expansion of the black dot, if necessary.

You may try visualising black objects instead of the preceding dot expansion – black cats, black dogs, black curtains, black boots, black skies. This is one of the techniques used by practitioners of the Bates' method of eye relaxation and sight improvement.

A technique worth holding in reserve is *paradoxical intention*, which has been known to work for stutterers. The stutterer deliberately tries to stutter, instead of struggling not to – and he finds he cannot stutter. So the insomniac may find that if he or she deliberately tries to stay awake, starting by trying to keep the eyes open, then sleep is stung into accepting the challenge. This is yet another example of relaxation being productive. By giving ourselves permission to stay awake, we are no longer tightened up over not being asleep. Then sleep comes. Attend alertly to the intermittent nocturnal sounds as they come to you – next thing you know it could be time to get up, wash and dress.

For some people getting to sleep and staying asleep is never a problem. The more relaxed a person is the less likely it is that he or she will have any sleep problems. When they arise, the approaches described above are almost certain to bring sleep. But occasionally nothing may seem, for the moment, to work. William Wordsworth faced that problem:

'A flock of sheep that leisurely pass by,
One after one; the sound of rain, and bees
Murmuring; the fall of rivers, winds and seas,
Smooth fields, white sheets of water, and pure sky;
I have thought of all by turns, and yet do lie
Sleepless!'

When you have tried a variety of techniques and nothing has worked this time: give up, get up, walk around the house for a few minutes. Make yourself a drink or spend a few minutes reading a book. You will not die; no calamity will descend on you. Very soon the urge to go back to bed will jump up; obey it, but forget about sleep. Here again the permission to stay awake nearly always brings sleep. The attitude of 'what happens, happens' is all important.

On awakening

This chapter has necessarily been taken up mostly by the problem of not sleeping. But when persons teach themselves to relax and to live a relaxed life there is rarely a sleeping problem. Go to sleep relaxed and you are almost certain to wake feeling restored, refreshed, and interested in what the new day will unfold. Your mood and what you feel, think, and do in the first minutes of a new day will have considerable influence on your emotions, thoughts, and actions during the hours ahead.

7

Meditation for Relaxation

A Western author writing a manual on relaxation before the 1960s would have been unlikely to include specific meditation techniques. But during the 1960s many thousands of Westerners, particularly Americans, discovered that sitting still in a quiet place and passively focussing their attention on a meditation object for about twenty minutes caused them to feel uncannily refreshed, physically and mentally. Now any book on relaxation that seeks to be comprehensive in describing methods of releasing stress should include the basic psychological devices of meditation. It is not necessary to include religious or doctrinal associations: the basic method, which is simple and direct, produces the relaxation response, and its effectiveness is not tied up with what William James called 'over-belief'.

The physiology of meditation

In the late 1960s and early 1970s, Drs Herbert Benson, Keith Wallace, and others in the United States investigated and published papers on the physiological correlates of the meditative state. There were similar studies of the physiology of meditation in Britain and in some European countries. Zen meditators were wired up and studied in Japan, and yogins in India. From the start it was clear that the practice of traditional forms of meditation could produce an extraordinary slowing down of body processes – a hypometabolic state distinct from those of deep sleep and hibernation – *a very relaxed state.*

A laboratory study of practitioners of Maharishi Mahesh Yogi's transcendental meditation (TM), a traditional Hindu yoga technique based on repetition of a thought sound, carried out by Benson and Wallace at Harvard Medical School towards the end of the 1960s, provided the first detailed knowledge of the many physiological changes that go with meditation.

Some of the meditators, whose ages ranged from seventeen to forty-one, had been meditating only a few weeks, others for several years. All recorded changes associated with deep relaxation.

The fall in metabolic rate was the most striking discovery. This was indicated by a dramatic drop in oxygen consumption within a few minutes of starting meditation. Consumption fell by up to twenty per cent below the normal level; below that experienced even in deep sleep. Meditators took on average two breaths less and one litre less air per minute. The meditators' heart rate was several beats less per minute.

During meditation blood pressure stayed at 'rather low levels' but fell markedly in persons starting meditation with abnormally high levels.

The meditators' skin resistance to an electrical current was measured. A fall in skin resistance is characteristic of anxiety and tension states; a rise indicates increased muscle relaxation. The finding was that though meditation is primarily a mental technique, it soon brings significantly improved muscle relaxation.

Meditation reduces activity in the nervous system. The parasympathetic branch of the autonomic or involuntary nervous system predominates. This is the branch responsible for calming us.

During anxiety and tension states there is a rise in the level of lactate in the blood. Lactate is a substance produced by metabolism in the skeletal muscles. During meditation blood lactate levels decreased at a rate four times faster than the rate of decrease in non-meditators resting lying on their backs or in the meditators themselves in pre-meditation resting.

The likely reason for the dramatic reduction in lactate production by meditators was indicated when further studies of meditators showed an increased blood flow during meditation – one of the few functions to increase in rate rather than decrease. Benson and Wallace found that there was a thirty-two per cent increase in forearm blood flow. Lactate production in the body is mainly in skeletal muscle tissue; during meditation the faster circulation brings a faster delivery of oxygen to the muscles and less lactate is produced.

The two investigators summed up the state produced by their meditating subjects as wakeful and hypometabolic. The physiological changes were different in many ways from those found in sleeping people or those in hypnotic trance states. Meditation, they said, produces 'a complex of responses that marks a highly relaxed state'. Moreover, the pattern of changes they observed in meditators suggested an integrated response, mediated by the central nervous system, of a similar reflexive nature as that which the Harvard physiologist Walter B. Cannon had called the 'fight or flight' or 'defensive alarm' reaction. Benson was later to call the changes he saw the 'relaxation response'.

Because we have scientific proof that the practice of basic meditation procedures elicits the valuable physiological changes of the relaxation response and because of the additional factors of its simplicity, practicality, and effortlessness, there are valid grounds for recommending that meditation be practised at least once daily, or twice daily, morning and evening, for ten to twenty minutes (preferably twenty minutes), in the best possible conditions of freedom from interruptions and distractions. The practice of meditation should be supported by the acquisition of skill in relaxation of the voluntary skeletal muscles, as taught in Chapter 3, and of dynamic or differential relaxation, as described in Chapter 4. These skills can become habitual.

What type of meditation?

It should be clear already that the type of meditation best suited for producing deep rest is different from that defined by the average dictionary; which still sticks to definitions based on what is known by the word in Christian spiritual training, in which meditation means thinking with concentration about some topic. We are using the word here in the Eastern sense, which may be viewed as the opposite of thinking about a topic, because it aims at becoming detached from thoughts and images and opening up silent gaps between them. It is this mind-quietening type of relaxation that is so effective in relaxation. It is not unknown in Christian mystical practice, where it is called 'contemplation'.

When we come to look at the basic psychological procedure at the heart of Eastern meditation and Christian contemplation, we begin to understand why prayer is relaxing, and why lying back and listening to music on radio or record player is relaxing; or focussing attention, while sitting still, on a fishing rod float; rapt gazing at a loved person, object, or scene; or fireside contemplation, like William Wordsworth, of 'the flapping of the flame'. . . . It is because all these things, and many more, involve staying still and passive attention to something.

In his book *The Relaxation Response*, Herbert Benson says that there are four elements basic to most traditional meditation, and these elements are those responsible for meditation's elicitation of the radical physiological changes of the relaxation response. These elements are:

A quiet place to meditate,
A comfortable or poised posture,
An object for attention-awareness to dwell upon,
A passive attitude.

This is my own preferred wording and order. Dr Benson says a quiet environment, an object to dwell upon, a passive attitude, and a comfortable position. Of the four basic elements, he says that a passive attitude is the most essential.

A quiet place
The best environment for the practice of meditation is similar to that most conducive to lying down or sitting to progressively relax the body muscles. Sit in a quiet place with minimum distractions. Later, you may be able to meditate well in places where more is going on: launderettes, railway stations, doctors' or dentists' waiting rooms, on trains and 'buses, and so on.

A comfortable or poised posture
A sitting posture is better for meditation than lying down. This is because lying down is the normal sleep position and meditation lying down could easily lead to sleep. If you are not a person who easily goes to sleep during the day, you may like to meditate in a

semi-reclining position on a sofa or large armchair with the back of your head supported. In traditional meditation postures, however, the back is normally kept erect, though not rigidly upright. I call this poised posture. The right attitude for meditation may itself be described as poised: alert yet also relaxed. Poised posture promotes the right state of attention-awareness for successful meditation. In the East the cross-legged postures, with head and back in vertical line, are considered ideal for meditation. I have described them in *Meditation*. They are worth mastering, but difficult and even painful at first for the majority of westerners. I have personally found what is usually called the Burmese posture very helpful. It can be mastered more quickly than the classic Lotus posture, in which the legs are crossed with feet on thighs, and imparts the right feeling of poised sitting for meditation. In Burmese posture the legs are not crossed but the knees are spread and stay down, and the legs are folded and the feet pulled back in front of the pelvis with one foot in front of the other. The 'cupped' hands rest at the tops of the thighs or on the heels. It is essential to have a firm cushion to sit on and a folded rug or blanket below that to prevent pain in the feet and ankles. The buttocks should be pushed out a little to bring the back into easy uprightness.

Considering that you spend up to twenty minutes sitting still in meditation, most readers will prefer to sit on a chair. In some chairs you can sit upright and have the back of your head supported; this is

Burmese posture

excellent. Placing a cushion against your back can ensure poised posture in sitting upright in some chairs in which otherwise poised sitting would be difficult. You can meditate, however, on a simple straight-backed chair by sitting in poised posture as described in Chapter 4. With hands on thighs, this may be called Egyptian posture. A good placing of the hands for meditation is to 'cup' them limply in your lap, with thumbs touching, with your wrists at the tops of your thighs.

An object to dwell upon

In Hindu Yoga the object the attention dwells on is often a *mantra*, usually a Sanskrit word or syllable. In Buddhism the focus for bare attention is often the meditator's own breathing. Both mantra meditation and awareness of breathing fulfil all the elements required for meditating for relaxation. Practitioners of transcendental meditation (TM) use a thought Sanskirt sound, and laboratory tests show that this practice has the capacity to elicit the relaxation response. Awareness of breathing works well also. And Dr Herbert Benson has employed a combination of the two meditative practices with hospital patients, who found it simple and effective to use.

Some meditation methods involve looking at objects with open eyes, but in the above two methods your eyes stay closed, which makes relaxation easier to induce.

Instructors in transcendental meditation make much of each person being given a mantra that suits his or her nervous system, but there does not appear to be any scientific support for this. Dr Benson concluded from his investigation into the physiology of meditation that though transcendental meditation works well in terms of eliciting the relaxation response, 'tests at the Thorndike Memorial Laboratory of Harvard have shown that a similar technique used with any sound or phrase or prayer or mantra brings forth the same physiologic changes noted during Transcendental Meditation . . .' He tells his patients to sit still, breathe calmly, and think the neutral word 'one' on each exhalation. It works well.

There is much to be said for choosing either a neutral word or a meaningless sound for mantra meditation. Some people, however, like to use a word like 'peace' which has relaxing associations. This is all right provided the word does not set off trains of associative thought. In this type of meditation the single thought-sound, repeated inwardly, has the effect of quietening the mind; Maharishi Mahesh Yogi says that the thought-sound takes the meditator to the source of thought. Studies of the brain wave patterns of meditators indicate that the deepest relaxation results when thoughts are absent, or few and of no importance.

If you make awareness of breathing your single meditation method, let your attention dwell on the gentle rise of your abdomen in diaphragmatic–abdominal breathing. Your breathing becomes very quiet and even after several minutes of meditation and the gentle movement and rhythm of abdominal breathing promotes relaxation.

A passive attitude or poised awareness

This last element of meditation for relaxation is said by Herbert Benson to be the most essential. I call it poised awareness or attention-awareness because in it relaxation and alertness are in perfect balance. There is nothing exotic about it: you were passively aware when you let go from tension in the muscles of your arms, legs, trunk, and face.

A passive attitude means that distractions from environmental sounds, skin tingles etc., and the inevitable intrusion into the mind of thoughts and images are viewed casually and detachedly. Let them come and go, of no more consequence than small clouds passing across an expanse of sky. But each time you become aware that your attention has slipped away from the mantra or the sensation of abdominal breathing, and you are engaging in a chain of logical thinking or developing interest in some sounds or other sensations, bring your attention and awareness back to the meditation object.

It is really very simple, as long as you keep a relaxed attitude going. Don't force, and don't cling. With practice, moments of great calm and deep restfulness during meditation will become more frequent.

In the Hollywood gangster movies of the 1930s there was often a gang member whose string of 'I thinks . . .' would be cut off by the gang boss with the menacing words: 'Know what your trouble is? You think too much!' Most of us do think too much. Oriental texts liken the mind to a cageful of monkeys and recommend meditation for greater peace of mind, and more cogent thinking when we really do need it. So much of our thinking, if we start looking at it, is unproductive and tension-producing.

Meditation has a special quality of awareness, a feeling tone that takes its colour mainly from a passive attitude. At least one writer on meditation – James Whitehill in *Enter the Quiet* – calls it 'relaxed awareness'. I am tempted to do the same, but have settled for poised awareness as there is no mistaking the balance between letting go and opening up and staying poised and aware. The prevailing attitude is passive, but there is a point where meditation proper slips into drowsiness or negative reverie. The right balance and tone is difficult to describe but easy to experience in practice. Note it well, for it may be used, as muscular relaxation and poise can be, in the midst of daily activity.

Calmness in everyday activities

'The criterion is that the meditator maintain a stable, relaxed, and alert attitude, whatever the mental focus', writes James Whitehill. A thought-sound for repetition silently in the mind and awareness of the sensations of breathing in the abdomen (its rise and fall) have been recommended as foci for meditative attention. These two methods have proved records for inducing deep relaxation and for bringing the many benefits in improved energy, efficiency, poise, and clarity of consciousness that many meditators have reported. Not least among the benefits are greater calmness in everyday activities. Deep relaxation from sitting practice lasts some time afterwards, and meditation's feeling tone and attitude may be employed even when you are active. You can be 'stable, relaxed, and alert' at most times.

Most meditators find that the practice of meditation increases the ability to become a witness of one's thoughts, sensations, and feelings. This can prove useful in coping better with negative thoughts and feelings, which lose much of their impact when viewed with a detached and relaxed attitude.

Once you become familiar with meditating, you find you naturally slow down and take time to look about you: to listen, touch, taste, and generally open up your senses to the 'what is' of the world about you. This is a positive gain. Even what are usually looked upon as 'ordinary' activities take on significance when responded to with poised attention-awareness. Which is why a Zen poet could exclaim: 'How marvellous this is! I carry water from the well. What a miracle! I chop wood for my fuel.'

8

Relaxation Therapy

A growing number of physicians and psychiatrists are using relaxation as an aid in the treatment of both physical and mental disorders. It is also used by some practitioners of the so-called 'alternative therapies', which should more accurately be looked on as complementary therapies.

In view of the damage to body and mind caused by stress, nervous excitement, and prolonged muscular contraction, the therapeutic use of deep relaxation techniques need not surprise us. However, it should be noted that relaxation therapy is rarely used on its own, but is usually supporting other treatment. The subject is extensive and can receive only cursory treatment here.

For the healthy person, relaxation helps maintain well-being and acts as a protection against illness. For the ill person, it acts in the direction of normalisation of body processes, which it does by freeing recuperative powers within the body itself. The energies released by relaxation, hitherto employed in supporting tension, now become free to aid nature and bring back health.

Relaxation is so basic to healthy living that it is doubtful if there is any illness which will not respond beneficially in some degree to its use, even if only through the relief of discomfort, pain, and anxiety.

When sleep is aided by relaxation skills, it improves in depth and quality and acts as a prime healer, more effectively carrying out its work of cell repair and renewal. That deep rest is therapeutic is shown by the fact that in severe illness nature herself prescribes deep and prolonged sleep.

The release of emotional tensions assist recovery of health in the body and is of special value to the neurotic personality.

When Eastern techniques of meditation, especially transcendental meditation, began to receive considerable publicity in the United States in the early 1960s, there was particular enthusiasm for meditation among college students. Some of these students were recruited by medical scientists working at university laboratories for studies of the physiological changes that occur during the practice of meditation. When the results were published, it was seen that the most obvious changes were those connected with a marked slowing down of body processes, such as oxygen consumption, heart rate, and electrical activity in the brain. Blood pressure went down when the pressure was above normal. And the skeletal muscles became much more relaxed.

The link between meditation and relaxation having been established, interest grew in other techniques of deep relaxation that had been in use. In fact, Jacobson's progressive relaxation, Schultz's autogenic training, and relaxation hypnosis had been in therapeutic use for nearly fifty years. Hypnosis, though not always using deep relaxation as part of the induction method, had a much longer history.

Therapeutic muscle relaxation

Edmund Jacobson introduced the idea of scientific muscle relaxation at Harvard University in 1909. Because of its scientific nature, progressive relaxation has appealed to physicians and to behavioural psychologists.

In his book *Progressive Relaxation* (1938) Dr Jacobson gave many examples of the therapeutic use of relaxation. He made a clinical investigation of muscular states to determine their significance in treating physical and mental disorders and achieved a direct and physiologic method – progressive relaxation – of quietening the activity of the nervous system. Several hundred patients received the relaxation treatment and improvement was noted in nearly all cases.

Marked or very marked improvement was observed in patients suffering from the following disorders: nervous tension, fatigue states, insomnia, anxiety states, depression, hypochondria, phobias, chronic colitis, oesophagus spasm, arterial hypertension, and tension headaches.

Considering the variety of disorders and the fact that treatment was often incomplete, the results proved the value of relaxation as a therapeutic aid. The patients' own reports upgraded the physician's results.

These results convinced Dr Jacobson that there was 'a widespread therapeutic opportunity for the method of intensive rest' and that the diminution of nervous tension aids the body's healing powers. The effect on the personality was to soothe and to promote those states of mind most conducive to recovery of health.

Studying the types of disorder which Dr Jacobson found progressive relaxation was best able to help, we see that it is likely to be effective as an aid in the treatment of illnesses in which stress and a psychosomatic element are prominent influences. Sedatives and medications were eliminated, and relaxation was the sole treatment Dr Jacobson used. He found relaxation helpful in psychotherapy. Whereas, in his experience, suggestion produced superficial results, relaxation seemed to get right down to the roots of the disorder.

Dr Jacobson also found relaxation training helpful in calming patients before and after operations.

The diseases and disorders for which muscle relaxation has proved of value are typical of those treated by other deep relaxation methods, such as meditation and hypnosis.

Hypnosis and self-hypnosis

The chief value of hypnotherapy is that the patient relaxes deeply and passively takes in and tends to actualise the suggestions of the hypnotist, or in self-hypnosis one's own instructions. The limitations are that some people do not appear to be hypnotisable and that others can reach only a very light trance state. However, a state of light hypnosis still may have therapeutic practicality, and it may be added that any state of deep relaxation offers an opportunity for attempting fruitful self-suggestion, either through speaking silently to oneself or by visualising success in some activity.

The history of hypnotherapy goes back to the earliest recorded medical history, and behaviour suggestive of the use of hypnosis appears in the history of folklore of the Druids, Celts, Africans, Chinese, and peoples of other cultures.

Hypnosis is a Greek word meaning 'sleep' – but when the physiology of the hypnotic state is gone into it is found that the state is not sleep in the normal meaning of the word; nor is it the same state as meditative consciousness. 'Ordinary' sleep is still largely a mystery, hypnotic sleep even more so.

Dr Herbert Benson lists hypnosis among methods that elicit the relaxation response. Present-day techniques of induction are mostly based on verbal suggestions of deep relaxation and 'sleep'. And hypnosis, including self-hypnosis, may be used directly to produce deep relaxation. The instructions given to the subject or to yourself are worded accordingly. An induction formula for self-hypnosis could open with the following words or something similar: 'I settle comfortably in the chair. Or: I lie on my back relaxed and comfortable. I close my eyes. I listen to my inner voice. I concentrate fully on what I am saying mentally. I think of nothing else. I am going to relax deeply. I am going to relax completely. I am going to sink into hypnotic sleep. I am going to enjoy refreshing relaxation and hypnotic sleep . . .' etc.

As hypnosis is not a technique that everyone can use effectively and because many people feel uneasy about its element of 'trance', I am not including a full description of the self-hypnosis technique in this book. (The opening words of an induction formula given above are taken to completion in *Relaxation East and West*.)

Hypnotherapy has a patchy record of results, probably because subjects vary in their degree of response to the induction method. Post-hypnotic suggestion has its therapeutic uses. The patient is told that he or she will behave in a certain way after the session of hypnosis has ended, and with the right subject this will come about. Sometimes by this method the symptom of a disorder is removed, but this should only be attempted when no harm could result to the patient in the light of any persisting underlying cause that needs to be treated.

Hypnosis is sometimes used as a substitute for an anaesthetic when other forms are not suitable for an individual or not available. Hypnosis is sometimes used in this way in dentistry, surgical operations, and childbirth.

The literature of hypnotherapy includes reports of treatment for skin disorders, high blood pressure, peptic ulcer, epilepsy, alcoholism, insomnia, phobias, sexual and other behavioural disorders. A frequent use of hypnosis is to eliminate unwanted habits like smoking, nail-biting, and facial mannerisms.

Autogenic training

This is another way of producing the relaxation response and obtaining its therapeutic benefits. It began as a method for bringing the kind of therapeutic techniques associated with hypnosis to more people. From the 1920s it has been used by many physicians and psychiatrists in continental European countries, especially in Germany and Switzerland. It is less well-known in Great Britain and the USA.

Though initially it is usually taught to a patient by a doctor, the patient learns to use it alone in a self-directed way. Its originator, Dr Johannes H. Schultz, called it autogene training. Autogene comes from two Greek words: *auto*, meaning 'self', and *genous*, meaning 'originated'. This indicates that it is intended as a self-help therapy, after initial instruction from a doctor. It is sometimes simply called autogenics. Like progressive muscle relaxation, it may be self-taught from reading books and used as a way to relax body and mind as well as being used for therapeutic auto-suggestion and imaginative exercises. Awareness is directed to the part of the body in most need of healing influence and healing is given pictorial expression in the mind and reinforced by positive self-talk. This may be done in a state of deep relaxation induced by any other method.

Some psychiatrists use autogenics to relax the patient deeply and to help release buried memories and feelings.

Parts of autogenic training resemble Yoga, or, updating the association, biofeedback. The trainee concentrates on certain physiologic functions which are normally regulated only by the autonomic or involuntary nervous system. The self-suggestions given are 'my right hand is becoming warmer' or 'my heartbeat is calm and strong'. Rises in hand temperature up to ten degrees Fahrenheit have been recorded in trainees. If you wish to try it, strap a thermometer to your hand, relax and see what you can do. The benefit of such Yogic-like control is to improve the circulation in areas where healing is required or pain to be relieved. Another place where warmth is suggested is the solar plexus, the network of nerves behind the stomach. Imaginative support is to think of warm sunlight spotlighting the area or a warm hand or hot water-bottle being placed on the stomach. Increasing body temperature in a body part is one of the controls facilitated by using monitoring biofeedback equipment. Some types of biofeedback machine give electrical signals for tension levels in the body muscles and offer a scientific way of learning muscle relaxation.

In the autogenic state a feeling of warmth suffuses the body, but the verbal formulae include an instruction 'forehead pleasantly cool' – Schultz called it 'a cool, deconcentrated head.' Perhaps he was familiar with a German proverb which says 'cool head, warm feet – that makes the best doctor poor.'

In autogenic training awareness is passive and poised, as it is in meditation. Autogenics is sometimes described as a meditation method: we might call it a relaxation–meditation method. Dr Karl Robert Rosa, in his book *Autogenic Training*, says: 'The subject, in the autogenic training state, is aware of himself in all his senses but does not reflect on himself.' These same words could be used of the meditative state; also Dr Rosa's description of autogenic training as 'the means to a new, relaxed enjoyment of one's pure existence.'

Biofeedback

Biofeedback also requires what has been described paradoxically as 'passive volition' to produce its conscious control over processes normally only regulated by the involuntary nervous system. Control is gained by the operator through using special electrical equipment to monitor fluctuations in body functions. Local control of temperature is one of its more dramatic achievements, as mentioned above. From the point of view of the person seeking increased relaxation, machines which signal the rise or fall of tension in body muscles offer a means of learning muscle relaxation, while other equipment which signals the presence of slow alpha waves in brain activity makes it possible to learn – the *how* is not fully understood – to mentally relax and enjoy what is sometimes described as 'electrical meditation'.

We are all familiar with feedback learning. As children, we learned to throw a ball straight at a target through a process of adjusting a throw in the light of the visual information of the ball going to one side or the other; in learning to talk, we listen to the signals of our parents' voices and on that basis make our own attempts; and so on. What is special about biofeedback machines is that they supply information on body processes of which otherwise we would have no knowledge. As the machines signal changes in these processes, we learn how to control them, though we may be mystified as to how we are doing it. How we actually do it we will not be able to say; but once again, as in muscle relaxation and meditation, it is all a matter of *awareness*.

Biofeedback was developed by medical scientists in the USA in the nineteen-sixties, at a time when the physiology of meditation was being studied. Progress was made when it was discovered that people could alter their brain rhythms when they were able to observe their signals on an electroencephalograph. The machines tend to be expensive for home use, but may be shared by groups. Once a control technique has been learned – in the case of relaxation usually quite quickly – the use of the machine is usually no longer necessary. Some people appreciate scientific confirmation of progress in a skill, but the goal should be to be independent of the machine. Most people can recognise when they feel relaxed without requiring to be wired up to any apparatus.

Meditation as therapy

From the use of meditation one would expect the kind of therapeutic results that one finds from the therapeutic use of progressive muscle relaxation, relaxation hypnosis, or autogenic training. Such is the case. However, meditation being a mental technique with wide-ranging physiological results, we may perhaps be prepared to anticipate some special influences at work.

The therapeutic benefits from meditation cannot be put down to any occult or mystical powers, but relate directly to meditation's elicitation of the relaxation response and its physiological correlates. Herbert Benson and Keith Wallace made what is now a classic study of volunteer practitioners of transcendental meditation, published in the *Scientific American* (1972). They concluded with the words: 'It should be well worthwhile to investigate the possibilities for clinical application of this state of wakeful rest and relaxation.'

This has been done and the results, as reported in many scientific papers, have been encouraging for the corrective and healing uses of basic meditation procedures. The Transcendental Meditation organisation have continued to invite investigation into the medical and social application of their type of meditation and numerous experimental studies have been carried out. Positive results were reported in the areas of normalising blood pressure, increasing learning ability, reducing anxiety, nervousness, irritability, depression, and neuroticism; eliminating dependence on alcohol, tobacco, and non-prescribed drugs; improving emotional stability in prisoners; strengthening the immune system and resistance to infectious diseases; a decrease or cessation of allergies; correction of sleeplessness, aggressiveness, etc.

Research into the changes associated with transcendental and other forms of yoga meditation and Japanese Zen Buddhist meditation suggest a successful use of meditation in the treatment of those disorders in which hyperactivity of the sympathetic nervous system could be a causative or exacerbating factor.

A notable feature of the reaction to meditation that suggests clinical application is the rapid fall in blood lactate levels, accompanied by an increased blood flow with expansion of the blood vessels. Researchers have found that there is a large rise in blood lactate in patients with anxiety neurosis and in persons under stress. And persons with high blood pressure have been found to have high blood lactate levels.

The practice of meditation relaxes the voluntary skeletal muscles; reduces the heart rate several beats per minute, so resting it; brings blood pressure down from unhealthy levels; and calms respiration, the nervous system, and the mind.

In Japan, meditation in the Zen Buddhist tradition is used as a treatment for mental disorders, and group meditation is practised by store and business staff to protect them against stress and fatigue. Medical scientists have made psychological and neurophysiological studies of Zen meditators. After twenty years of such studies, Dr Tomio Hirai reported, in *Zen and the Mind: Scientific Approach to Zen Practice*, that Zen sitting meditation (*zazen*) influenced both body and mind in ways that could be used therapeutically. 'Scientifically,' he wrote, 'it can be shown that Zen meditation regulates the whole organism of the body internally and externally.'

Meditation, he goes on to say, regulates the operation of the involuntary nervous system and removes tensions affecting the controlling cerebral cortex. It promotes a healthy body and 'a smooth, well-ordered state of mind'. He cites the German psychopathologist Karl Jaspers who said that all kinds of meditation 'share a distinctive mental action: training for the sake of operation on consciousness in such a way as to work a relaxing change in it.' The change is effected whether or not one believes in the tenets of Buddhism, Christianity, or any other religion. The results of the meditation procedure is to relax the mind, and this clearly has therapeutic value. Dr Hirai studied the brain wave patterns of meditating Zen monks and found that they indicated a calm state of mind that was conducive to psycho-physical health. The Zen meditator is not asleep, he pointed out, but 'filled with abundant vitality'.

A major factor in the mind–body buckling under stress is a failure of adaptability. Research has shown that the practice of meditation improves the adaptability of the nervous system, so that it copes well with change, and that it fosters healthy, stable functioning of the nervous system.

Basic meditative procedure neutralises stress automatically, regardless of the nature of the meditator's beliefs. The therapeutic benefits of meditation are open to all patients prepared to practise its simple techniques.

Sleep therapy

Sleep therapy is used in the USSR and in some other European countries. Though to this day sleep remains mainly a mystery, we do know that during sleep the body's powers of regeneration and healing are mobilised.

At a sanatorium specialising in sleep therapy near Berchtesgaden, in the Bavarian Alps, the method employed by the medical director is to alternate three or four days' sleep with a similar period of normal wakefulness and sleep, repeating the process three times in all. Positive results are claimed in cases of migraine, hay fever, asthma, influenza, meningitis, and poliomyelitis; but most encouraging of all have been the results in the 'stress' disorders, such as stomach ulcers, insomnia, psychosomatic complaints, alcoholism, high blood pressure and neurosis. The patients are roused periodically for feeding and hygiene; food consumption is reduced considerably.

The treatment in the early stages is not always as pleasant as it sounds. The first periods of wakefulness may be accompanied by pain or depression; and in the cases of neurotic patients problems hitherto hidden below surface consciousness now emerge into its light and have to be faced and firmly grasped. But these are signs, say the sanatorium doctors, that a cure is at work, the bursting of the boil before healing is possible. The doctors report that in deep sleep patients often sort out their problems and awake (in more senses than one) to at least a partial resolution of inner conflicts.

Music therapy

Music is used in many countries to supplement other therapies. It helps calm and integrate the activities of the nervous system. Listening to music, and participating rhythmically through song and dance, relaxes physical and psychological tensions. The music is carefully chosen to suit each patient: soothing music for one, lively for another. Nervous and emotional disorders may respond well to music therapy.

Painting is another artistic therapy that may help heal the troubled mind, and which, like musical expression, is creatively relaxing for any person engaging in it as a leisure activity.

Stress-related health problems

Aches and pains
In the common complaints of muscular aches and pains we may see examples of how emotional stress produces physical symptoms.

Disease of a joint or bone can be responsible for abnormal states of tension or spasm in some body muscles. There the muscular action is protective, for it immobilises the diseased part. Emotional stress is usually responsible for more general muscle tension, though key areas may be most obviously contracted – such as the forehead, jaw, neck, hands and lower back. Aches and pains arise when muscles are tensed for prolonged periods.

'There may be some justification for the recognition of what may

conveniently be termed a psychosomatic tension state or syndrome', wrote Dr Maurice Parsonage, a British neurologist, in his
contribution to *Postural and Relaxation Training in Physiotherapy
and Physical Education* (1968). He also wrote: 'In the case of the
chronically anxious and tense individual it appears that much of his
bodily musculature may exhibit persistently increased tension, as if
in preparation for motor activity which is either inhibited or does
not find a satisfactory outlet.' Dr Parsonage recommends that the
psychosomatic tension syndrome should be treated by a combination of psychotherapy and relaxation therapy.

Tension headaches
Tension headaches are of various types. The muscles of the forehead, scalp and neck become taut. The pain may spread from the
neck upwards to the back of the head; it may feel like a weight
resting on the top of the head; it may be an ache above the eyes; or it
may feel as though tight bands press against the temples.

Drs D. Cox, A. Freundlich and R. Meyer, of the University of
Louisville Psychology Clinic, experimented with the use of muscle
relaxation in the treatment of patients suffering severe headaches.
One group received only the pretence of treatment: they were given
a dummy tablet, but told that it was an effective muscle-relaxant. A
second group was taught how to relax their muscles in a verbal
instruction course of eight lessons. They were told to use their new
relaxation skills at the first signs of a headache beginning. A third
group also learned to relax their skeletal muscles, but they learned
with the aid of biofeedback equipment. Electrodes were attached to
the patients' frontalis muscles, which are in the forehead and which
usually tighten during severe headaches. The biofeedback machine
emitted bleeps when the frontalis muscles tensed and quietened on
their being relaxed. This third group of patients learned to control
the bleeps and the amount of tension in their forehead muscles.

The patients were told to keep a diary record of headaches they
suffered and to rate the severity of each attack. The placebo
(dummy) group showed a slight reduction in the severity of the
headaches that occurred, an indication that suggestibility could be a
therapeutic factor. But considerable reduction of pain occurred in
the patients in the two groups who had been given sessions of

instruction in relaxation. The groups who learned relaxation skills by verbal instruction and those using biofeedback machines did about equally well.

Blood pressure and heart disease

High blood pressure is considered to be a 'disorder of civilisation'; which is to say that it became more of a problem as the pace and pressures of life increased in this century. It is easily raised by nervous excitement, and it rises alarmingly when a person gets very angry or worked up over a situation or issue.

Stress threatens the heart through raising blood pressure. Do you consider the expression 'broken heart' only a fictional figure of speech? Researchers from the Tavistock Institute of Human Relations, London, found that grief could kill. They studied the records of 4486 widowers for nine years after their wives had died in 1957. Within the first six months of their wives' deaths 213 of the men died – nearly one-and-a-half times more than the rate for married men of the same age. And the biggest death-rate increase was from heart attacks and heart diseases, which killed 101 of them.

Most research has sought the causes of heart attack in the modern diet. Detailed analyses of diets, cholesterol levels in the blood, and deaths from heart attacks show that a diet low in saturated (animal) fats (fifteen to twenty per cent) and low in blood cholesterol reduces the risk of heart disease. But in some countries whose national diet is high in cholesterol, heart attacks are relatively low. In such countries it is believed that regular exercise may be a factor in keeping the arteries from being clogged up by fatty substances. But many researchers also believe that a happy relaxed disposition acts as a safeguard against heart disease.

Some researchers believe they have established a link between stress and cholesterol in the blood. Stress, they say, exaggerates the effects of cholesterol.

People who work in jobs where the strain on the emotions is high have a higher heart attack rate than people with less stressful jobs.

What all the evidence points to is that the best way to protect your heart is to keep your diet low in saturated fats, take regular exercise, and stay relaxed and cheerful as much as possible.

Psychosomatic disorders

Techniques of muscular relaxation and meditation may bring relief or cure in psychosomatic disorders – those in which emotional disturbances are causing bodily symptoms. This is a controversial area in which it is difficult to gauge how far a psychological factor is responsible for an illness. It is widely believed that emotional stress can be responsible for asthma, high blood pressure (hypertension), migraine, menstrual disturbances, peptic ulcer, and many other disorders; but these can also be purely medical conditions. Relaxation therapy will usually bring relief and may sometimes end a disorder, but for a complete cure it is usually necessary to end the emotional tension that is at the root of the problem.

Anxiety states, phobias and neurotic disturbances

This is an area of human distress and disorder that may be tackled with the use of relaxation techniques. Many psychiatrists are using relaxation therapy in the treatment of phobic disorders. Fear's more ubiquitous and sophisticated variation – anxiety – may also be counteracted through relaxation methods, and this is something of interest to every person, for anxiety seizes us all sometimes. The problem of coping well with tension-producing emotions is of great importance to any persons suffering distress because of them and any person interested in more relaxed living. A new chapter will deal specifically with this topic.

9

Coping with Emotional Stress

Anger and fear, though of great utility to our hunting forefathers, may now be described as negative and self-destructive emotions in relation to their most frequent expression. This is for reasons connected with unnecessary and over-prolonged activation of the alarm or fight or flight response mechanism. These emotions are rarely experienced in their full rawness in current civilised life. What is doing most damage to body–mind health and efficiency are more sophisticated variations of anger and fear, such as feelings of enmity, envy, frustration, ego-sensitivity, anxiety, unease, disquiet, guilt, and so on.

Anger and fear/hostility and anxiety are at the heart of destructive emotions. Perhaps we should have said anger–fear/hostility–anxiety: some psychologists say the two go together, though one may predominate in the manifestation of feeling. This fits in with their sharing the same physiological arousal of the autonomic nervous system. In some feelings the presence of both anger and anxiety are clearly perceived. In guilt, for example, there is anger directed against oneself and also a measure of fearfulness.

Personality type, which some investigators believe is inherited to some extent, has a bearing on whether or not the anger or fear ends of the stress-response continuum predominate. Anger is most often seen in extraverts, the fear or flight side in introverts. Extraverts are active, impulsive, sociable, the direction of their interests outwards; introverts are careful, thoughtful, reserved, the direction of their interests often inwards. Extraverts when emotionally unstable tend to become aggressive, excitable, changeable, and restless; introverts become anxious, unsociable, and depressed. Studies indicate that highly emotional extraverts tend to suffer from hysteria, psychopathy, personality disorders, and criminality. Anxiety states, phobias, obsessive–compulsive disorders, and depression are mainly found in introverts.

Both extraverts and introverts benefit from learning how to relax. Introverts have the greater patience for staying still long enough to benefit from neuromuscular relaxation or meditation; the impulsive restless nature of the extravert is opposed to immobility. Extraverts should, however, persist in learning to relax well, to the point where just a few minutes letting go show good results; for they have their quickness to anger and their impulsiveness, restlessness, and excitability to control.

Both heredity and environmental influences are factors in people becoming tense, anxious, etc. Heredity can hand out a predisposition to buckle under easily to stress in situations where other people show no alarm reactions. But the more resistant types also suffer stress when a considerable weight of pressure and perceived threat is put upon them.

If we can reduce anger and fear, and their sophisticated variations, to a minimum and cope with them well when they do arise, we will be taking a major step towards relaxed living. The relaxation techniques already described will lay the foundations for balanced living, and may be supported by any methods for coping with stressful emotions that are found to be helpful individually. We will be looking for something more than the 'coping devices' which are built into the organism: crying, cursing, laughter, sighing, talking, etc. Much of value for everyone can be learned from looking at techniques used by psychiatrists and psychotherapists to tame severe attacks of fear and anxiety. Also worth looking at are the methods which experienced athletes, sportspersons, and public performers of all kinds employ to overcome efficiency-destroying anxiety and nervousness.

Anger and enmity

Anger is the most immediately dangerous of emotions. Many heart attacks are brought on by a fierce flare up of anger, and sometimes by anger directed against oneself, as in the story of Nabal told in

Samuel, Book 1, Chapter 25. William Harvey, who reported in a book published in 1628 'that blood circulated round the body from the arteries to the veins under the action of the heart', in the same book gave the case history of a 'strong man who, having received an injury and affront from one more powerful than himself, and upon whom he could not have his revenge, was so overcome with hatred and spite and passion, that at last he fell into a strong distemper, suffering from extreme oppression and pain of the heart and breast'. About 1700, the English surgeon John Hunter said: 'My life is at the mercy of any fool who shall put me in a passion.' He died abruptly during a meeting of the board of governors of his hospital.

Consider what is happening when a person becomes angry. Blood pressure soars and the body prepares for attack. There is a flow of adrenalin and other energy-summoning chemicals into the blood-stream. Blood leaves the organs of digestion and goes to the muscles. We perceive signs of mobilisation for fight in a tightening of the muscles of the face, trunk, and limbs. The eyes bulge, the face contorts and reddens, veins stand out on the forehead. The hands are squeezed into fists and the muscles of the arms contract. The angry person presents an intimidating appearance that warns: watch out!

If the arousal is brief and the energy mobilised is spent in vigorous action, as it was in its original primitive functioning, little if any harm is done. But such is the nature of current civilised life that nearly all eruptions of anger have to be restrained and contained, perhaps left smouldering and unexpressed for hours at a stretch.

Today anger is rarely helpful, but on the contrary is highly destructive in interpersonal and social relationships. It is, as Horace said, a brief madness. Is madness ever helpful? It may be argued convincingly that even in those rare situations in modern life where aggression is permissible – the soldier in war, the boxer in a championship fight, etc. – a very strong case can be made out for survival or victory going to the person who stays cool, calm, and collected and who does not succumb to wild, hasty, or poorly coordinated actions.

Anger most often arises through some thwarting of our ego interests, some blow to self-esteem, or some threat, insult, or damage to our possessions, which may include family, race, country, occupation, political party, cherished cause, or favourite football team or entertainer. In situations where this is likely to happen we can learn to perceive the danger quickly and to relax physically and mentally. It is important to see the worth of not being the victim either of anger or of egoistic hypersensitivity.

Relaxed attitudes contribute to preventing an anger response arising and that is a point at which the problem of this and other destructive emotions may be effectively tackled. What we perceive as threats to our physical or ego selves, or to our prized possessions or earnest expectations, will trigger anger or fear, but relaxed attitudes, such as tolerance, forgiveness, acceptance, and love, accompanying body–mind relaxation, mean that events which before were allowed to cause tension and stress no longer do so. There is no alarm reaction because there is no longer a perception of threat.

Intolerance and prejudice frequently cause anger and tension. Tolerance of other people's actions and beliefs is promoted by seeing how both are likely to be the product of their conditioning, just as our own are likely to be also the product of a complex conditioning and set of influences.

A psychological technique that makes for less friction and more relaxation is, without sacrificing your own deeply held views, to mentally stand in an opponent's ideological shoes and see, to some extent at least, why he thinks and feels as he does. There is an instructive game worth playing – you briefly switch places with an opponent on some issue and express his or her view as sincerely, skilfully, and ardently as you can. Doing this may not change your opinion, but afterwards you cannot usually hate your opponent and you are left with some understanding of his or her viewpoint.

Anger is assuaged and tolerance, forgiveness, and other relaxed attitudes are fostered by taking a 'broad view' in matters of beliefs and interpersonal disputes. We will return to this later.

The following questions are worth asking yourself and answering. What kinds of people make you feel angry and tense? Name specific persons who irritate you or arouse feelings of hostility. Think of ways in which you could learn to appreciate their better qualities, find them more interesting, or modify the features in them that make you angry, irritable, hostile, tense. What can you do when you talk to them, work with them, cannot avoid their company, that would prevent a tense response arising?

One answer is to find something humorous in the situation. Social life will become more relaxed and enjoyable if you can see people with a humorous and tolerant eye, such as that which has made Beryl Cook such a popular artist in Britain.

Fear and anxiety

Fear and anxiety are the major sources of psychological distress in modern life. Fear is responsible for the escape side of the fight-or-flight reaction. Actually there are two responses in extreme fear: adrenalin-fuelled running away or freezing and incapacity to move, a response which some animals use to advantage. A person or animal may freeze momentarily, then start running. In the course of current civilised life the experience of raw fear is infrequent, whereas that of anxiety is commonplace. It is often said that we live in the age of anxiety.

What distinctions can be drawn between fear and anxiety? Fear is a primary primitive emotion, whereas anxiety is a more sophisticated and subtle variation. We do not say that animals are 'anxious' but that they are 'afraid'. Fear is an essential element in anxiety. It may precede anxiety or charge in and dominate it for short periods. Fear is usually short-lived, but anxiety is often prolonged, undermining health in the ways described in Chapter 1. Fear is a more direct and powerful emotion than anxiety. That anxiety feels more subtle than fear is in large part due to its being less overwhelming and cerebral than fear; anxiety is often a subconscious emotion. When anxiety burrows into the unconscious mind and stays there, the muscle tension that goes with it becomes continuous, waking or sleeping. Fear usually has causes that can be easily discerned and described, whereas the causes of anxiety are often difficult to discern and describe.

There is an anticipatory element in anxiety. We feel highly uncomfortable about some coming encounter or event about which we experience doubt. We experience thoughts and images of some threat to our physical and/or ego selves. We may not be exactly sure what the painful event is going to be like, or it may take several possible forms with which the imagination plays. The person anxious about sitting an examination may anticipate being confronted by questions that are difficult to answer; images of how parents will react to failing the exam may swim into mind; or there may be anticipation of the actual experience of fear–anxiety during the examination: the churning stomach, the sweating palms, the thought-inhibiting spasms of dismay. The public performer may have visions of doing badly and of the agonised feelings that would then be experienced during and after the performance. We can become fearful about fear and anxious about anxiety, so that the distress is intensified and reinforced.

Psychiatrists speak of 'free-floating anxiety', meaning a feeling of unease whose causes cannot be articulated. Dr Karen Horney's concept of 'basic anxiety' will be described shortly. Some existentialist thinkers have said that being human – having minds that can reflect on the human condition and human mortality – entails a permanent, deep-rooted, ontological anxiety or *agnst*.

The threat of annihilation for all or much of the human race through nuclear war is an ongoing threat responsible for widespread anxiety, and for some people eruptions of fear, even panic, when the mind dwells on the possible nuclear holocaust.

The signs of acute fear are usually visible: the subject's pupils dilate, the body muscles contract and the posture is squeezed in as though trying to contract into as small a target as possible – the opposite of the expansive, muscle loose posture of relaxation. Anxiety betrays itself only in small signs: restlessness, irritability, twitchings, nail biting, and so on. It can often be successfully hidden from others: muscles are tensed, but not so strongly as with fear, and the distress is mostly in the feelings and in the mind.

It is surely significant that the English language has a large number of words meaning subject to anxiety and closely related feelings – apprehensive, concerned, disquieted, troubled, unnerved, upset, unsettled, and so on. So rich a vocabulary for anxiety feelings points to their being an important area of experience for English-speaking people. But how necessary are they?

It may be argued that fear and anxiety are normal and helpful responses when they are based on realistic assessments of threat and that they contribute to human survival and effectiveness by arousing motivation for taking counteraction to remove or avoid a threat. However, it may also be argued that any such usefulness is only present when fear and anxiety are not so powerful that they are incapacitating and impairing judgment, and we may even be justified in wondering if they have any value at all to mature adults.

Instinctive fear is probably protective in children and in the 'second childhood' of extreme old age, but in the in-between years, if we have our wits about us, fear, anxiety, and other emotions in the fear group are of doubtful value. We can recognise dangers and cope with them best with bodies free from tensions ana minds not agitated by fearful or anxious thoughts. Edmund Burke wrote: 'No passion so effectively robs the mind of all its powers of acting and reasoning as fear.'

Experiencing fear or anxiety to the point of partial paralysis of body and mind is clearly a disadvantage in coping with a threat, and it is clear also that most people experience levels of fear and anxiety, and other fear-based feelings, that are responsible for needless muscle tension, needless inner churning, needless wastage of energy, needless negative thinking, and needless suffering.

Unnecessary though most experiences of anxiety may be, the subjective distress and the concomitant physiological changes are real enough. This includes the symptoms and distress of persons suffering from the neuroses.

Neuroses

The term *neuroses* permits a variety of definitions. It was first used in the second half of the eighteenth century to describe diseases of the nervous system, and then in the nineteenth century to describe 'functional disorders' – functional disturbances of the nervous system without structural changes. This definition still appears in dictionaries. However, Freud and the psychoanalysts have used the term to describe disorders of the personality – mental disorders which cannot be attributed to diseases of the nervous system. To behaviourists, on the other hand, the problems of neurotic disorders are ones of learned behaviour and treatment a matter of learning different behaviour. There is also the popular usage of the term 'neurotic' to refer to a person who is manifestly tense, anxious, 'nervy', and emotionally unstable, or behaving unpredictably, irrationally, irrelevantly, and so on.

The *psychoses* present much more serious problems than the neuroses. Many investigators believe that the former are due to chemical malfunctioning, but psychoanalysts look for the roots of the problems in dynamic forces within the psyche. Neurotic people are not usually called insane, but psychotic persons are considered to be *non compos mentis*. A distinction is drawn between organic and functional psychoses. The organic psychoses are caused by organic diseases, mostly of the brain, but organic diseases are not usually associated with functional psychoses, such as schizophrenia, manic-depression, and paranoia. Anxiety states and obsessional thoughts are neurotic symptoms; persecution mania and severe hallucinations are psychotic symptoms. In psychosis the disruption of the normal course of existence is usually severe, and the psychotic's perception of reality is more disturbed than that of the neurotic.

The difference between the psychotic person and the 'normal' person is not difficult to see, but the dividing line between the neurotic person and the 'normal' person is not easy to draw. Whether or not a person is labelled 'neurotic' is a question of degree. The personality of the neurotic person is not completely different from that of the so-called normal person. It can be said that *every* person displays irrational behaviour and emotional instability on occasions or will admit sometimes having neurotic impulses and feelings. Neuroticism has to badly disrupt the normal course of existence for it to reach the stage where professional treatment is necessary.

If we are all neurotic to some degree or at certain times then the plight of people diagnosed as suffering neuroses and the methods used to treat them should be of interest to us: there could be helpful lessons to be learned.

Psychotherapeutic methods

Traditional psychoanalytic and psychiatric methods often contain an element of induced relaxation. It is not without significance that the classic position for the patient in psychoanalysis is reclining on a couch, and some prominent psychoanalytic techniques – free association, for example – may be linked with relaxation. In free association, words and images are encouraged to flow spontaneously. Some therapists teach patients to relax deeply and then engage in guided reverie, lucid dreams, etc. Other psychotherapeutic techniques aim for a release of pent-up feelings, which may have accumulated because of some traumatic experience or stressful relationship. Therapists guide patients to acceptance of neurotic complexes and conflicts, acceptance and self-understanding leading to improvement or cure.

Basic anxiety

Some people have inner conflicts, unconscious anxieties or deep-rooted psychological problems that need to be worked through, either by self-analysis or with professional help, before the full benefits of relaxed living can be realised. Relaxation practices will help by freeing energies and calming the mind's turbulence sufficiently for positive action to be taken to face, understand, and eliminate sources of psychic tensions.

Some psychoanalysts and psychiatrists believe that many people develop a basic anxiety in childhood which may continue to trouble them in adulthood. If basic anxiety is pronounced, the musculature will reflect the underlying psychic tension and some form of rigidity in behaviour will be present.

Psychoanalyst Karen Horney's account of basic anxiety was particularly comprehensive and clear, and her whole approach to the neuroses was based on it. She defined basic anxiety as 'a feeling of helplessness toward a potentially hostile world' or 'the feeling a child has of being isolated and helpless in a potentially hostile world.' Basic anxiety is the root of neurotic disturbances which take their forms through neurotic persons' ways of tackling feelings of insecurity carried over from childhood.

Most people overcome it, at least sufficiently for it not to be a problem in adult life. But for some men and women basic anxiety is the root of neurotic manifestations, which take such forms as excessive self-assertion (moving against others), excessive submission (moving toward others), or excessive withdrawal (moving away from others).

Though neurotic trends are ways of easing the pressure from basic anxiety, they create conflicts that set up tensions. An example is the person who wants to withdraw from others yet also wants to be popular and much loved, or successful in a way that necessitates contact with others. Neurotic trends are at best partial and inadequate. They are harmful because they produce rigidity and immobility in the personality. They have a compulsory character. They work to some extent, but usually with unfortunate consequences. Neurotic solutions to the problem of basic insecurity nearly always lead to the clash of contradictory drives within the psyche, to psychophysical tensions and psychosomatic problems. When defensive techniques fail to work, anxiety becomes acute.

Understanding the consequences of neurotic defensive positions and trends leads to a lessening of their rigidity and of anxiety. It becomes possible to be more adventurous, to adopt friendlier attitudes toward other people, and to feel more grateful for being alive. As already shown, it pays to face fears and anxieties and to teach yourself to relax and work your way through them.

Karen Horney said that neurotic strategies for coping with basic anxiety could be studied and worked through as they exist as present problems, and it was not necessary to probe to uncover their causes in relationships with parents or other childhood influences. The effect of this type of analysis and bond-loosening is that the individual becomes more spontaneous, more freely and fully functioning, more himself or herself. Karen Horney's 'real person' turns out to be the 'relaxed/poised person' in the deepest psychological sense. The human condition does not allow for problems to be ended once and for all; but false problems can be dropped and genuine problems are no longer crippling and a dreadful drain on energies and resources.

Rigidities and anxieties shackle the natural faculty for enjoyment of existence; relaxing defensive rigidities helps set this faculty free. In concluding her book *New Ways in Psychoanalysis*, Karen Horney wrote: 'In my judgement, freeing the patient from anxiety is only a means to an end. The end is to help him to regain his spontaneity, to find his measurements of value in himself, in short, to give him the courage to be himself.'

Phobias

Most fear and anxiety experienced in modern civilised life is unnecessary and destructive rather than helpful. We have dramatic examples of this in people who are the victims of phobias. In seeing how psychiatrists and psychotherapists overcome abnormal fears in their patients we can learn some things about removing or reducing those unnecessary fears and bouts of anxiety which seize most people from time to time.

An exaggerated fear/anxiety response is seen in the phobias, which are triggered by specific situations. Some people, to an abnormal degree, fear contracting a fatal disease, storms, heights, spiders, travelling in aeroplanes, and so on. There are names for all the excessive fears psychiatrists treat. *Claustrophobia*, fear of confined places, is a familiar word to lay persons, but *agoraphobia*, fear of going out of the house and to shops, libraries, restaurants, theatres and other public places, is the most common phobic syndrome.

The term agoraphobia was first used by a German psychiatrist, Westphal, about a hundred years ago to describe the states of dread or anxiety suffered by some of his patients when faced with having to leave their homes and walk through streets and squares. The Greek word *agora* means an assembly, or market place; *phobos* means fear. The agoraphobic suffers an acute alarm reaction on going out into streets and shops, on public transport (though not usually in his or her own car) such as 'buses, trains, and aeroplanes (but aerophobia is an abnormal fear of draughts), on mingling with crowds, though also when confronted with open, empty landscapes.

The agoraphobic may summon sufficient courage to go to a theatre or cinema, but have to sit in an aisle seat convenient for a quick escape if an attack of panic comes on.

There are some mysteries about the disorder. Why is it that children rarely suffer from it? It usually develops in the late teens, the twenties or thirties. Two-thirds of agoraphobics are women. Some dramatic experience or crisis may be the start of it – an accident, a bereavement, a miscarriage, an embarrassment suffered in a shop, hairdressers, restaurant, theatre, etc. But it may also develop slowly, with no obvious reason for the loss of confidence.

Agoraphobics are often helped by carrying a comforting object in a pocket or handbag.

The severity of the syndrome varies between individuals and in individuals at different times, which leads people erroneously to jump to the conclusion that the agoraphobic only needs to 'get a grip' on himself or herself to 'snap out of it'. Many agoraphobics are virtually housebound. More women suffer severely from this disorder than men and may disguise their problem behind the phrase 'attachment to the home'. Even when the problem is severe, the sufferer may overcome it momentarily if the motivation is strong. I knew a man who left his bedsitter on less than a score occasions over a period of eighteen years which terminated with his death. On each outing he was driven by the craving for nicotine. Normally his cigarettes were bought for him, but very occasionally he ran out of them. If by leaning out of the third-floor window he was unable to find a person to make the purchase, after twenty to thirty minutes of torment he would undertake a fearful dash to the nearest stockist of cigarettes, make the purchase, and race home in alarm. But, as explained, such adventures were extremely rare.

A writer with a long-established reputation as a humorist has devised, he tells me, a test for agoraphobics which proves the insubstantiality of their illness. Place one hundred pounds in the centre of a large field, which the agoraphobic can have on summoning the courage to collect it.

Probably most agoraphobics would make the dash and lift the money – many might even do so to grab a lesser amount. But this would not dispel the agoraphobic's anxiety states; the disorder would remain. Progress can be made in lessening the psychophysical distress of the agoraphobic by less eccentric methods.

Many victims of fear of public places 'soldier on' without seeking medical help, or they may report it to their doctor in general terms and be prescribed tranquillisers. Professional treatment is beneficial, and in many cases self-help for phobics is practicable once they know how to go about it.

Desensitisation procedures

In the treatment of phobic disorders behavioural methods have the highest record of success. Behaviourism is often attacked on the grounds that it is too mechanistic, denying the psyche, the soul, the spiritual, and so on. Whatever the rights and wrongs of disputes between behaviourists, psychoanalysts (Freudians, Neo-Freudians, Jungians, Adlerians, etc.), humanistic and existentialist psychiatrists and psychotherapists, there seems nothing, in the wider view, that can be said against taking an eclectic approach to therapy. Each of the main types of mind-healing therapy are probably well suited for the treatment of particular problems and particular cases. The behavioural approach, which says that fears have been conditioned and can be deconditioned, is well equipped for dealing with phobias.

Behavioural therapeutic principles and methods are simple, and the lay person can easily adapt the methods to self-help treatment. If that does not work, then professional help should be sought.

When fear is unreasonable and excessive, there is the possibility of confronting and overcoming it. This may be done gradually or by a head-on encounter. The former is the most used therapeutic approach and psychiatrists call the procedure *desensitisation*.

Note that aversions are not phobias. A person may go goose-pimply every time chalk squeaks on a blackboard, but will not be frightened by a piece of chalk or a blackboard. Some phobic fears do seem ludicrous to the great majority of other people. Hippocrates was intrigued by a man with a fear of flutes when heard at night but not in daytime; he also mentions a man afraid of heights who was afraid even when standing beside shallow ditches.

Most phobic disorders may seem ridiculous to most people, but it does not alter the emotional experience or the courage needed for deliberate confrontation during the desensitisation process. Persons physically crippled receive general public sympathy, but the phobic's disorder being psychological, the sufferer receives the kind of lack of sympathy and misunderstanding generally given to neurotics. Yet phobics need courage to deliberately face emotional turbulence which they recognise as irrational.

The courage of phobics and of persons who suffer attacks of anxiety is known mainly only to other sufferers from these psychophysical states. They will appreciate a story told by Viktor Frankl, the existentialist psychologist. It is related by Dr Isaac M. Marks, a psychiatrist who uses behavioural methods, in his book *Living With Fear: Understanding and Coping with Anxiety*. The anecdote illustrates the importance of taking the right attitude or inner posture in coping with fear and anxiety. In the front line during the First World War, a Jewish military doctor in the Austrian Army was sitting beside a colonel when a heavy bombardment began. 'You are afraid, aren't you?' said the colonel to the doctor; 'Just another proof that the Aryan race is superior to the Semitic one.' 'Sure I am afraid,' the doctor replied, 'but if you, my dear Colonel, were as afraid as I am, you would have run away long ago.'

The desensitisation procedure is the main behaviourist therapeutic approach to phobias, anxiety states, obsessive compulsion, sexual problems, etc. The theory behind it is that the patient's problem has been conditioned or learned, and the circumstances of first learning it are of little importance compared with the task of deconditioning the conditioning, desensitising the sensitising, and substituting neutral, relaxed feelings for fearful, tense feelings.

If a phobia is very powerful, the first exposures or confrontations with the feared thing or situation may be on a small scale, perhaps even only in imagination, the patient first being taught to relax as deeply as possible. Relaxation softens arousal and makes it possible for stronger exposure to be instigated, including confrontation with the phobic situation in actuality and not just before the mind's eye. For example, if the fear is of cats, the desensitisation process starts with the patient relaxing and looking at photographs of cats or cats conjured up in the mind's own cinema. Later the patient stays as relaxed as possible while observing a cat or cats, eventually is able to stroke a cat, and finally to have one sit in his or her lap without anxiety. The desensitisation process is gradual.

A technique which requires much courage but which has the merit of shortening the time necessary for desensitisation is not to undergo a series of gradually advancing exposures but instead to 'jump in at the deep end' at once with a major confrontation of a feared thing or situation. An agoraphobic may sit in a public square or other public place for perhaps an hour. The therapist may give support by accompanying the patient on the first occasion or two. The technique is called *flooding*, and three or four such powerful exposures may produce a radical change in the patient's tolerance of such situations.

The techniques of gradual desensitisation (especially) and flooding lend themselves to self-help use by many sufferers from phobic disorders, anxiety states, etc.

Modelling is the most recent of the major behavioural techniques. It was pioneered by Professor Albert Bandura of Stanford University, in California. He found that difficult children became more relaxed and cooperative in play on being shown films of children of their own age group playing together without being aggressive. And seeing films of children behaving confidently in certain situations helps build confidence in observing children who have been fearful and anxious in similar situations.

The same procedure is helpful for adults. A man or woman with a compulsion–obsession, for example, will be shown films of men and/or women engaged in normal behaviour and are then encouraged to emulate it.

The modelling method can be used in conjunction with the gradual desensitisation procedure or other therapeutic methods.

Another favourite treatment method of behavioural psychologists is *positive self-talk*. Self-talk is what you say to yourself, or, if you like, what you are thinking. We think largely in words. Sometimes people can be seen moving their lips as accompaniment to an interior monologue.

What you say to yourself can be helpful or unhelpful, stress reducing or stress intensifying, in any situation. If you are angry, the things you say to yourself are usually those which support your anger: 'I feel furious with myself! . . . I could kill that bully/bitch/crook/villain! . . . Everything has gone wrong. I might have known this would happen . . .' If you feel fearful, the natural tendency is to reinforce the fear with negative self-talk, such as: 'I'm scared stiff . . . I'm trembling all over . . . If I make a mistake here, I'm in real trouble . . . This person/creature/situation turns me into a quaking mass of jelly . . . My stomach is churning like a washing machine . . . I hate this terrible feeling.' If you are anxious, the natural tendency is to add to your anxiety by carrying on a negative interior monologue: 'I just know the event that lies ahead is going to turn out to be a disaster . . . I'm almost certain to fail . . . I'm sure to make a mistake . . . I can't think clearly . . . My mind feels agitated and confused . . . My palms and forehead feel sweaty . . . People can see how anxious I am . . . This is ridiculous . . .'

Note that most of the problem with negative self-talk is the pessimistic appraisal of the situation. Perceptions and judgments are unhelpful. Note also that attention dwells on unpleasant body sensations and on images and verbalised thoughts of failure, of embarrassment, of humiliation, of disaster, of the worst happening.

Positive self-talk, on the other hand, is encouraging, reassuring, and stress reducing; it builds confidence and creates calmness. It also turns the direction of attention away from body sensations and pessimistic thoughts to the tasks in hand. In the jargon of the psychologists, the aim is to be task-oriented rather than self-oriented, with thoughts of 'Now I do this. Now I do that.'

Relaxation is also favoured by self-talk that promotes relaxing attitudes: for example, 'Everybody makes mistakes. Let's keep going calmly. Don't rush. Give yourself plenty of time.'

The wording of your positive thoughts should be natural to you and should include statements that reflect any thoughts or things that can be done that you have found helpful in past experience. For example, if you suffer from agoraphobia, you may have found that you feel less distress while travelling alone by train if you direct your attention to the passing scene, as seen through the carriage window. If so, your self-talk on the journey should include reminding yourself to let your attention dwell on points of interest seen beyond the carriage windows. It is also helpful to remind yourself not to hurry, to let time pass, to accept and to float or flow, or give yourself any other inward instructions that reduce stress and promote open awareness. This is positive thinking or self-talk.

Positive statements made silently to yourself should always be realistic. For example, when you are gripped by the physiological changes of fear or anxiety, to tell yourself 'I am not the least bit afraid or anxious' is to ask for the rejoinder: 'Oh, yes you are!' That is unrealistic self-talk. Realistic, yet positive and helpful, self-talk is to say to yourself: 'These sensations I am feeling are unpleasant but will not harm me seriously. If I accept them, I can free my attention to attend to what needs to be done. I can direct my attention outwards to tasks in hand. I can let go, float and flow. Etc.'

Remembering to relax and to use positive self-talk prevents anger, anxiety, or any other stressful emotion that is gathering strength to cause confused thought and unpredictable behaviour.

Phobic disorders may produce such unpleasant feelings that some sufferers start fearing that they are going mad. In such cases professional help is advisable. They are not going mad, but suffer fear to an extent that most people know only rarely in extreme situations, if ever. Treatment rarely requires admission to hospital. The majority of people with phobic problems should be able to reduce them to manageable size or even effect a complete cure through a determined effort at desensitisation with relaxation, with or without professional help.

Social phobias
These occur about equally in men and women and develop mostly between the ages of fifteen and twenty-five. They may develop

slowly or arise rapidly out of an embarrassing or humiliating incident. Blushing may accompany sweating and other symptoms of acute anxiety, augmenting the feelings of inferiority, low self-esteem, and poor self-image usual with this phobia.

A social situation is the phobic event: being introduced to people, entering a crowded room, attending parties, etc. Sitting opposite another person on a train may be agonising: the gaze of others is feared. There may be exaggerated self-consciousness about some physical characteristic – a large nose, large or small breasts, facial skin blemishes, and so on.

In the social context desensitisation means progressively bolder exposures to social situations, increasing confidence and relaxation in such situations. Here again, in severe cases the feared situations may be tackled at first in imagination. The patient lies down or sits still, relaxes, then visualises himself or herself having a meal alone in a restaurant, having a drink in a crowded bar, meeting new people at a party, and so on. The next step is starting to face the actual situations that cause acute anxiety. Each individual sufferer is the person in the best position to determine in the desensitisation process what provides a slightly tougher confrontation.

Confidence in social situations is gained through learning the ritualistic skills they require. Most people come to handle them more or less adequately through learning what best to do and say, having observed what experienced practitioners do and say. The social phobic's inner distress and tension prevent satisfactory learning of social skills.

Most social phobias result from inferiority feelings, shyness, etc. The sufferer is often an introvert, but introversion *per se* is not a disorder or disease. Most of the world's greatest artists, writers, and composers have been introverts, some of them socially withdrawn. The work of Hans Eysenck and others indicate that introverts and extraverts are distinct psychological types but each capable of making valuable contributions to civilised society. What counts most is whether introverts and extraverts are stable or unstable personalities. It is possible to stay an introvert and not be straitjacketed by withdrawal compulsions. The healthy introvert may read books or listen to gramophone records in preference to going to parties, but the relaxed introvert could go at any time to a party and get the most out of it in talking to people, observing people, etc.

Sexual behaviour also has its rituals which can be learned through experience, when the individual is not crippled by fear and anxiety. The procedure in correcting sexual fears, inhibitions, shyness, and the functional problems they cause, is on similar lines to that already described for coping with social and other phobic situations.

Problems of obsession–compulsion may also be treated successfully by the graduated exposure method. An example is the person who cannot touch objects that have been touched by other people without immediately washing his hands; he is encouraged by the therapist to do so until the difficulty is overcome.

Anxiety states

Anxiety states and depression are the two commonest psychiatric disorders. Anxiety state or neurosis is sometimes chronic, but more often it is recurrent and bouts last minutes, hours, or days. The usual symptoms are racing heart, palpitations, sweating, dizziness, nervousness, etc. Panic attacks may come without warning and seemingly without reason. When there is no apparent reason for an attack of anxiety it is sometimes called free-floating anxiety.

Anxiety states are unpleasant yet without any advantage. Normally we are prepared to put up with some discomfort and distress if it serves a useful purpose, but knowing that one is suffering anxiety to no purpose adds to the existing distress. Moreover, it erodes confidence and impairs performance in any task. The problem is exacerbated by feelings of anger at oneself and embarrassment at the thought of what others may see and think. Anxiety attacks make sensitive, intelligent people feel like idiots.

The physical sensations of an attack of anxiety are not as noticeable to others as the sufferers usually believe they are; nor are they as serious a matter to the sufferers themselves as they rate them on the subjective evidence. If the physical sensations – faster heart rate and breathing, 'butterflies' in the stomach, trembling, sweating, etc. – are observed as objectively as possible, with as much detachment as can be summoned, they are seen to be sensations of no great importance *in themselves*; it is the ego-sensitive, self-tormenting way of responding to them that causes the distress. If the negative psychological reaction can be converted into a more positive response, or the sensations be accepted simply for what they are, then the painfulness of anxiety can be ameliorated immediately.

Accepting and floating

Dr Claire Weekes, honorary consultant physician to a hospital in Sydney, Australia, has helped many sufferers from phobic disorders, anxiety states and all those states covered by the popular diagnosis 'nerves', by methods primarily requiring changes in attitudes: from those causing stress to those producing relaxation. 'Accept and float' summarises her approach. The tricks the nervous system plays when it becomes hypersensitive can be overcome, she says, by letting go and accepting whatever sensations come, by relaxing to and going with feelings instead of fighting them, which is what most people do, making the symptoms worse instead of better.

She says that what are called 'nervous breakdowns' arise from sensitisation and not from any breakdown in the functioning of the nerves. A nervous breakdown is the incapacitating exhaustion that follows a period of great strain. Nervous breakdowns can occur to anybody if the pressure is severe enough, but some people fall victim more readily than others. The person who suffers a collapse of reasonably effective functioning is highly sensitised to stress. According to Dr Weekes, the main damage is done when the sufferer becomes highly afraid of his or her fear. The additional fear, a reaction to a reaction, activates the adrenals to produce even more adrenalin and the body to react even more strongly to the loudly ringing alarm bells. The sufferer is trapped in a fear–adrenalin–fear cycle, with an enormous expenditure of energy that eventually leads to exhaustion and incapacitation.

The problems which are popularly called 'nerves' or 'nervous illness' arise because a state of sensitisation of the sympathetic nervous system leads to nervous hyperactivity and stress prolonged to intolerable lengths. The sufferer is hypersensitive to situations perceived as stressful, and to noise, bustle and other stimuli which most people can cope with most of the time. Sometimes sensitisation arises because of an experience of severe stress, such as an accident or a bereavement, but it more often develops gradually because of a prolonged emotional crisis: guilt, shame, a battle between equally weighted tendencies, and so on. The way to peace for the sensitised is through some form of desensitisation.

Desensitisation procedures used by behavioural therapists have already been described. These were progressive exposures to feared situations, the powerful, courageous confrontation called flooding, and acquiring calmer habits from seeing models of what the patient wishes to become.

The ability to let go from tensions in the skeletal muscles and to quieten the mind with meditative techniques also serves to reduce nervous sensitivity and hyperactivity.

Dr Weekes' treatment is based on the capacity a change of attitudes has to quieten the body's alarm reactions and also to prevent their arousal. Body–mind relaxation is combined with relaxed attitudes to acceptance and of letting time pass without trying to arrest it. Dr Weekes summarises the beneficial changes in attitudes as *facing*, *accepting*, *floating* and *letting time pass*.

Note the opposites to these attitudes. The first two are respectively running away and fighting – the stress reaction partnership. The opposite attitude to floating is arresting and 'listening in'; and the opposite to letting time pass is being impatient and trying to force recovery at an impossible and unnatural rate.

What Dr Weekes asks her patients to face, accept and float past, without being pressed by time, are the physical sensations of fear and nervous excitation: the nasty feeling in the pit of the stomach, the palpitations, the trembling, the sweating palms, or whatever happens to arise. The main problem for people suffering from phobic and anxiety states is that they become so resistant to the sensations they experience. The severity of these physiological changes may be dramatically reduced by not tensely flinching from them or fighting to suppress them, but by *accepting* them, by having the sense of floating or reacting freely, and by letting time flow without becoming impatient, so that tensions and problems can dissolve and go in their own time. You overthrow your difficulties, eventually, by submission, in a kind of psychological judo.

It is necessary for patients to accept that they will have to live with uncomfortable sensations for some time, but they can do so in the knowledge that they will fade away eventually if they are starved of the fearful attention that keeps them active and strong. In time the attention will more and more find alternative foci of interest and body sensations will be noticed less and less. Patient acceptance is the key to recovery.

Important in Dr Weekes' therapeutic approach is what she calls 'floating'. Fighting creates tension, floating relaxes. In her book *Self-help For Your Nerves*, Dr Weekes tells of a patient who had been unable to enter a shop for months. Her efforts – and she did try to force herself – to enter a shop led to paralysis and failure. Dr Weekes advised the patient not to force, not to fight; instead, she should imagine she was floating 'on a cloud' into the shop. At the same time any thought that could become an obstacle was to be allowed to float out of her head. The patient was successful immediately in applying the changed-attitude method.

How can a simple word – 'floating' – achieve so much? Because the word represents a thought and with the thought goes a feeling. A few minutes of self-observation will show how feelings go with particular thoughts. Fighting a fear makes a person tense, and tension inhibits action. But thinking and feeling 'floating' is relaxing and helps action.

Floating means letting go, mentally lying back as though cushioned by a calm sea. It means non-resistance, going with the feelings that come, whatever they may be. You can float through tense sensations or you can let them float through you. It is not apathetic surrender, but a positive acceptance that has the power to alter reactions controlled by the involuntary nervous system. Meeting your problems with real acceptance, with floating, and with patience, will change sensations.

You do not have to imagine that you are floating on a cloud. Any imagery that helps give a sense of relaxed ease may be used; or you may simply think and feel 'floating'. And instead of imagining obstructive thoughts floating out of the mind without giving them respectful attention, an alternative is to imagine yourself floating past obstructive thoughts.

It is a matter of loosening attitudes: let what comes in the way of sensations come and having come, accept them as of no great importance. Remember that relaxation comes through *not* doing anything. Dr Weekes says that we should wait for relaxation, not strive for it. Tension and fear that are floated past or that float past us and are starved of attention soon start fading away. Indifference will be easier if we busy ourselves with objective tasks. In psychologists' jargon, your attention will be other-directed rather than self-directed. Meaningful work takes us away from our anxieties and troublesome desires and thoughts.

With relaxed attitudes, recovery will come if time is allowed for the body to regain its internal harmony. Remember that the type of person who allows time to exert nearly constant pressure is a prime candidate for a heart attack or a stress disease.

Acceptance is the key to success with Claire Weekes' therapy, but it has to be genuine acceptance and not a teeth-clamped stoicism.

Paradoxical intention

We are so used to resisting unpleasant feelings and unwelcome reactions that Dr Weekes' treatment by accepting or reacting freely seems revolutionary. Dr Viktor Frankl, a psychiatrist belonging to the existentialist school, goes even further with his psychotherapeutic technique called 'paradoxical intention'.

In this method you do more than fully accept your emotions and physical sensations – you try to intensify them. If your problem is being unnecessarily afraid, then you deliberately tremble and try to feel as frightened as possible; if your problem is stammering, you deliberately try to stammer instead of fighting to correct it; if your problem is blushing, then you try to blush your hardest.

Amazingly, this approach often has the effect of making what you are trying to do impossible. You cease being afraid; you are unable to stammer, or to blush. Or you may still do these things but with more of a 'who cares?' attitude, so that the problem starts disappearing.

Here again, letting go or relaxation is an essential factor in the success of the technique. Trembling, stammering, blushing or whatever the problem may be, is brought onto a more conscious level than hitherto by being freely acted out. The more wholehearted the performance, the better the chances of therapeutic success. For example, the fearful person should shake and shudder in an exaggerated way – like the conductor with a quivering style who at his first-ever rehearsal with the orchestra of La Scala, Milan, was comforted by the principal violinist with a whispered: 'Coraggio [courage], maestro!'

Paradoxical intention does not work for all emotional and behavioural problems, but it has been used successfully for a number of them.

Stress immunisation

Dr Don Meichenbaum, a Canadian psychologist, believes that we can make ourselves immune to most of the stress that occurs in certain situations by a kind of 'inoculation' procedure. You build up resistance to the situation by imagining it, by rehearsing it, replacing negative statements with positive statements on the lines described earlier in this chapter. Dr Meichenbaum says we should prepare for a potentially stressful situation by composing and rehearsing positive self-talk statements we will use, wording them in a style consistent with our own vocabulary and personality. He advises that we remind ourselves to stay in the present and remember what it is that we have to do. As mentioned earlier in relation to social phobias, there is a ritual for most recurring situations and the more times you perform it the easier it becomes. So: know the ritual, prepare for it, even rehearse it. What physical movements have to be performed? What are the things that may be said? To know the answers to these questions is to make a good beginning in preparing for self-management of anxiety.

Experiments give grounds for believing that rehearsed exposure to emotional stress will prepare people to cope better with the real thing. For example, some children in the United States were given mock examinations of their teeth and they showed less fear on actual examination by dentists than children who had not been emotionally 'inoculated'.

What, of course, is involved is a form of desensitisation. The rehearsal amounted to a mild confrontation of the feared situation and lessened its impact when it came.

College students who had prepared in imagination for enduring a tourniquet on their arm were able to last out twice as long as unprepared students. Preparation included relaxing muscles and being aware of breathing slowly and deeply. While keeping their muscles loose, the students were advised to think of other things than the pain: to do some mental arithmetic (subtracting sevens from one-hundred in order); to see what was to be seen through the window; to count the tiles on the ceiling; to dispassionately study the changes of colour in the swollen arm. An alternative technique was to imagine lying on a beach with the sun warming the tourniqueted arm, or to imagine that the arm has been given a local anaesthetic and is numb and feels no pain.

For possibly stressful situations, we can also prepare in advance and have suitable ritual, positive self-talk, and imaginative techniques ready for use.

These methods of coping with anxiety come together in the practical experience of skilled public performers, whether on a sports field or track or on a theatre stage or concert platform. Calmness under pressure will be discussed in Chapter 10.

Cognitive control

As relaxation practice proceeds, you will find that your attitudes start to change in helpful ways and that the destructive emotions become weaker and arise less frequently. This process can be helped along by keeping firmly in mind awareness of the harm done by unnecessary emotional tension. Become aware of your most characteristic negative emotions and of the situations in which they occur, and become aware particularly of the early warning signs of their appearance. If our lives depended on it, we could control our anger, fear, etc. We can do it in less dramatic circumstances. We can check the expression of emotions if something important is at stake: for example, if showing what we really feel about an employer would probably lead to instant dismissal. Each time a negative emotion does not arise, we save energy, avoid harm to the organism, and strengthen control.

Note that these emotions arise in *us*, and they only appear when we perceive some threat, frustration, or insult. Learned relaxation techniques give cognitive control solid support. Don't expect the elimination of negative emotions in all circumstances. Sometimes you may feel that you are taking steps backwards and are even more troubled by stressful emotions than before. There is a reason for this: because you have become more aware of your emotions, they figure more prominently in consciousness. It is an emotional parallel of the way sitting still and directing your attention into your mind in the early stages of meditation makes you more aware of the crowds of thoughts that are normally there, so that at times you feel that you are not doing very well at cultivating mental silence. With patience, just as the number of thoughts in your mind will be reduced by meditation practice, so too your emotional turbulence will be lessened by relaxing more, by understanding the problem of harmful feelings, and by awareness of them. Awareness in itself can in time tame the more strident emotions, just as it dissolves tension in body muscles in relaxation sessions.

See the danger coming and, in time, often the emotion will not arise at all. Through practice in subtle observation and cognitive control we can learn to check the cause of the expression of negative emotions. Self-observation reveals that our most harmful and needless emotions always appear in association with certain thoughts. Self-observation also shows that these thoughts are expressed in silent inner speech. This self-talk can be rephrased to produce relaxation and equanimity rather than anger, envy, anxiety, etc. Another important advance is to see how the feelings you have are connected with specific patterns of thinking, with specific attitudes and points of view. Here again, relaxation practices supported by positive self-talk and imagery can effect changes in attitudes and beliefs, which become more conducive to relaxed/poised living.

If you feel yourself tensing up, you should learn to take relaxation measures instantly, thus preventing the worry–anxiety spiral gathering force, a whirl of apprehensive self-talk and imagery. Instead, view awareness of the first signs of tension as the signal to let go from it, physically and mentally. Fighting or trying to suppress the tension will only heighten it; it feeds on effort because it is a form of straining itself. By now you should be familiar with the feeling of letting go from tension, which you will have discovered has nothing to do with *trying* to relax.

It is a mistake to believe that worry will do any good, that somehow the gravity of any situation makes it essential to go in for troubled thinking and gloomy brooding. The best strategy is creative thinking, followed by action in the world out there, not inside your mind, where sojourns should be brief. If the situation is such that nothing can be done about it, then a wise acceptance is the best policy.

Relaxation practice makes us realise the extent to which awareness, attention calmly and gently focussed, has the capacity to dissolve tensions. If even for a few seconds you can shift aside the imaginative film which you mentally superimpose on the physical sensations of your emotions and focus attention on the sensations themselves, you will be surprised to find that little or no emotion remains, only a few unimportant physical sensations. What our imaginations add is much worse than the physiological changes, the bare machinery of the emotion. This is an instructive lesson and one worth recalling when faced with an unpleasant emotion.

Bare attention of this kind is a meditative technique, and requires an element of detachment, of an observing 'I'. The practices of neuromuscular relaxation and of meditation will help you find a calm centre in yourself out of which you will often be able to function even in difficult situations.

10

Calmness under Pressure

This chapter is concerned mainly with stress and performance in athletics and sports, but most of what will be said will apply equally to giving of one's best in artistic performances of all kinds. Acting, singing, speaking, dancing, playing a musical instrument, and so on, are themselves physical activities, whose success depends in large measure on not losing poise on important occasions. The evaluation of importance belongs to the individual participant.

It is in sports and arts requiring delicacy of touch that we see the most disastrous consequences of anxiety and muscle tensions. Snooker is an example of this: even the top professional players sometimes falter on an easy shot because the cue arm 'seizes up' (there is unnecessary muscle tension). This happens when the pressure is on, as in a tight finish to a match. Sportsmen use various expressions to describe the harmful effects anxiety can have at crucial moments in their sports: 'choke' and 'freeze' are two of them.

In general, it is the competitor who has learned to perform smoothly and efficiently, whatever the pressures, who gets to the top, assuming always that there are also the necessary advanced skills. The same thing can be said of public performers in the arts. Nervous tension has prevented some highly talented men and women having the distinguished public careers their artistry warranted. Vladimir Horovitz, no less, did not play the piano in public for some years because he feared it would involve excruciating nervous excitement.

Psychological preparation

Brent S. Rushdall, professor of coaching science at the School of Physical Education and Outdoor Recreation, Lakehead University, Ontario, has made a study of stress in competitive sport. He discovered that psychological preparation is as important as physical training if an athlete is to realise his or her full potential. Many talented athletes and sportspersons fail to give of their best when it comes to the big occasion, for reasons essentially similar to those which can mar the performance of singers, dancers, pianists, public speakers, and so on.

Dr Rushdall and colleagues studied groups of world-ranked athletes in ten Olympic sports. They discovered that the athletes who regularly gave of their best on the most important occasions displayed certain behaviours and characteristics both before and during competition. Dr Rushdall gives an account of these in his book *Psyching in Sport*.

Summarised, the main competition behaviours and characteristics of top performers are:

They give their maximum effort and intensity in competition.

They enter competition equipped with a detailed plan.

Their competition plans include provision for things not going as normally expected.

They prefer to be alone shortly before a competition.

They prefer to warm-up by themselves, and include in the warm-ups some of the movements to be carried out in competition.

They concentrate on what they are going to do and put aside thoughts of other competitors (though these may have been thought about in the planning stage).

They view nervous arousal as something to be controlled and directed into high levels of performance.

They are able to gauge the amount of arousal that is just right for their best performance, and if they go above it they are able to regain composure.

They are confident, and this is a key factor: if lost before a contest, it is quickly recovered.

Mental rehearsals precede competitive performance.

In the lead-up to performance, concentration on the coming
   contest is total.
They assess their coming performance accurately. A runner
   knows what his or her time is likely to be over the distance run,
   a thrower the length of his or her throw.
They are not easily distracted by unusual or unforeseen circumstances before or during competitions.
They do well even in unfamiliar arenas.
They are able to handle well small distractions and all kinds of
   stressors likely to occur before competitions.

We see here a re-run of points made in the preceding chapter
about how best to cope with anxiety situations. Elite athletes have
relaxation skills, monitoring their levels of arousal. Their attention
is firmly on the tasks in hand (they are task-oriented). Their
thoughts give confidence (positive self-talk).

Actual competition behaviours and characteristics of top athletes
include:

Total commitment.
One-pointed concentration on the stages of performance.
Concentration on technique when tired, which has the effect of
   directing attention away from sensations of fatigue.
Giving of one's best even when losing a race/event/match.
Coping well with pressure, such as a close finish.
Learning from performances, the feedback going into planning
   for the next performance.

Arousal and anxiety

Experienced athletes learn to harness the force of an appropriate
'psyching up' emotion, which is a state of arousal that is not
connected with the tensions of the state of anxiety. The amount of
arousal that is helpful depends on the activities engaged in. Vigorous physical activity, such as the explosive sprints, throwing events,
weight-lifting, etc., can benefit from high arousal levels, but playing
snooker or giving a piano recital will be helped only by lower and
finely controlled arousal.

An acquired ability to let go from tension can be employed

usefully to control arousal levels that have risen too high prior to competitive activity or which have peaked too soon.

The commencement of the build-up of arousal varies from two weeks to two hours before an event. It is important for the athlete's efficiency that physiological arousal should be accompanied by appropriate mental activity, with attention focussed on 'task-specific factors' (i.e. what needs to be done).

Studies show clearly the harmful effects of anxiety on both preparation and performance in athletics, sports, and games. It tenses muscles that need to be relaxed, disrupts smoothness and rhythm, makes control of arousal difficult if not impossible, and causes mental confusion.

Anxiety is mainly due to how impending competitive situations are perceived, appraised, and talked about inwardly (negative self-talk). Here again, self-oriented thinking does damage, whereas task-oriented thinking is helpful. The state of mind of the performer in the few minutes prior to performance can be crucial. Highly anxious performers are easily distracted, easily lose confidence, easily lose the rhythms of technique, and easily allow the mind to be invaded by irrelevant thoughts.

Dr Rushdall and other experts on the most effective preparation for athletic or other competitive performance advise ways of eliminating anxiety prior to and during performance that are essentially those that were underscored in Chapter 9:

Relaxation sessions, accompanied by positive imagery.
Concentration on whatever needs to be done in preparation and during a performance (task-oriented thinking and attention).
Knowing what needs to be done and ritualising it, so that it comes easily and automatically.
Rehearsing the ritual prior to performance.
Finding appropriate levels of arousal and controlling arousal.

Relaxation and the performer

Relaxation is clearly valuable in the preparation for an important performance, at all its stages, and it also plays an important part – as active or dynamic relaxation – in the actual event prepared for. Differential relaxation was discussed in an earlier chapter. Reference was made earlier also to the Zen approach to sports and to creative arts, in which relaxation and strength combine in a poised way.

It is part of the preparation of top athletes in Eastern Europe that they have a session of relaxation, which is combined with positive imagery, two hours before a competitive event. They also use relaxation skills to control arousal levels. Each athlete has a base level of arousal just before competition, and the relaxation period establishes a constant level of arousal from which to tune up.

Athletes warm-up in the minutes before competition. Some of the warming-up movements should simulate those required for the competitive activity itself. Shaking the limbs loosely is a frequent warming-up practice and throws off some unwanted tension, if it should be present, in the musculature.

The focus of attention should be narrowed on the actions to be carried out, with distractions kept to a minimum, as in the practice of meditation. Performance may be mentally rehearsed, moving smoothly through its stages without lingering over any one point of technique.

Many athletes find positive self-talk helpful in the minutes before an event and perhaps during it. Some tennis players may be heard to express their self-talk aloud between and during games. In 1975, Dr Don Meichenbaum and D. Turk presented a paper on 'The cognitive–behavioural management of anxiety, anger and pain' at the Seventh Banff International Conference on Behaviour Modification, in which they said that 'how you think is how you perform'. In athlete's self-talk key words can trigger the activity desired – power, speed, agility, stability, and so on. Each competitor should settle on the most effective words to use. A tiring athlete's thoughts should be on technique as well as on effort, for fatigue can cause technique to falter. Exhortations to oneself to 'come on!', 'get a move on!', and so on, should be linked carefully with the level of arousal a particular sport or performance can best take.

A chanted word (mantra?) from the spectators can lift athletic performance and bring new life into tired limbs. Emil Zatopek must have been helped greatly by the chant in unison of 'Zatopek! Zatopek!' from thousands of spectators for his triple gold medal success at the Helsinki Olympic Games.

Arthur Ashe sat immobile, eyes closed, and meditated between games on his way to a famous title win at Wimbledon. This was an example of relaxation being used in the rest intervals of a competitive sport.

It not infrequently happens that an inferior player believes that a tennis match is lost, and inferior psychologically gives up but keeps up the learned movements. His or her anxiety having evaporated with acceptance of defeat, the 'underdog' relaxes and starts playing with smoothness, a flowing rhythm, and surprising effectiveness. But what happens then? More often than not the pattern is this: The better player momentarily becomes anxious, loses his or her smooth rhythm, indulges in negative self-talk – 'I know I'm a better player than my opponent. Now he/she is getting on top. Defeat would be humiliating.' However, the inferior player suddenly feels shock at his/her success, tenses up again, and as crucial points are reached, finally falters. Meanwhile the better player, if experienced, calms down, replaces negative thoughts with positive self-talk, and goes on to win.

The preceding scenario applies equally to contests between two players in other sports, and sometimes between whole teams.

Poised performance depends on differential relaxation, on economy of effort and movement, contracting those muscles essential for the task, relaxing those not needed. Most great boxers, footballers, swimmers, swordsmen, tennis players, etc. demonstrate these points, as do most distinguished dancers, pianists, violinists, etc. Occasionally you find performers who get to the top in spite of some elements of awkwardness, but these are the exceptions that prove the rules.

11

Changing Attitudes:
A Wise Relaxation

Pam, an English woman who is the central figure in Alan Sillitoe's novel *Her Victory*, has an accident while driving a car in a European country. Afterwards, she muses: 'Why I turned left instead of right I'll never know. I was happy and unthinking, a wrong state of mind because how can you be responsible if you are so stupidly relaxed? You have to pay for the air you breathe by being vigilant all the time, no matter how wearing.'

It should be perfectly clear by now that the relaxation skills learned from this book are not incompatible with either alertness or responsibility; on the contrary, they improve efficiency, with economy of effort, in driving a car or in any other activity. They can aid creativity. William Wordsworth spoke for all highly creative people when he spoke of 'a wise passiveness'. In this concluding section we will touch on some psychological factors contributing to what might be called 'a wise relaxation', primarily the influence of *attitudes*.

Attitudes and beliefs

The problem of stress – though this is easily missed – is in large measure a question of which attitudes and beliefs you prevalently hold. Attitudes are inner postures or stances responsible for the patterns of your thinking, and so for your feelings – feelings are linked with thoughts.

'Human beings can alter their lives by altering their attitudes of mind', wrote William James, the American philosopher and psychologist. By adopting new attitudes you can change, at a stroke, whole constellations and dynamic patterns of thought.

Note that attitudes and beliefs are something that *you hold*. The influence of cultural conditioning is strong, but most people feel that there is some element of choice in these matters. Through our attitudes, we determine largely whether or not living in general will be enjoyed or become a misery. The popular saying 'life is what you make it' reflects a wisdom expressed by many great thinkers and spiritual teachers throughout the ages.

'The aphorism, "As a man thinketh in his heart, so is he", embraces the whole of a man's being', wrote James Allen. 'It is so comprehensive that it reaches out to every condition and circumstance of life. A man is literally what he thinks. His character is the sum of all his thoughts.'

'The mind is its own place, and in itself can make a heav'n of hell, a hell of heav'n', was how Milton put it. Shakespeare was even more concise: 'There is nothing either good or bad, but thinking makes it so.' And Ralph Waldo Emerson: 'Nothing can bring you peace but yourself.'

How we interpret what is happening to us or what might happen to us decides how stressful or freely flowing life is going to be. This certainly applies for most people most of the time – and even the shock of overwhelming misfortunes can be softened by the victims' choice of attitudes.

Dr Viktor Frankl noticed that the men and women most likely to survive the horrors of a Nazi concentration camp were those whose attitudes directed their thoughts to things valuable and worth doing if and when liberation came. He developed an existentialist psychotherapy based on helping patients find *meaning* in their lives.

The main problem with inspirational writing about positive thinking of James Allen's kind is that the effects often start fading from the mind soon after reading the words. The same applies to the warm emotion of religious conversion. In a minority of cases the altered thinking lasts, in both instances. However, body–mind relaxation pacifies the nervous system and promotes healthier attitudes and beliefs, and at the same time healthy attitudes and beliefs make psycho-physical relaxation easier to achieve and to sustain.

Many of the relaxation techniques described in Chapters 9 and 10 owe their effectiveness to changing from tension-producing attitudes and beliefs to those in which threats, insults, and blows to self-worth are no longer perceived.

Life does not have to be 'wearing', even when alertness and responsibility stay strong: on the contrary, relaxation contributes inestimably to opening up to life in full awareness and to finding pleasure, significance, and meaning in life's multifarious sensations, experiences, and relationships.

Support for this view comes from the life work of Abraham H. Maslow, a humanistic psychologist who studied the most mentally healthy people he could find. The characteristics and values of those people accord almost fully with the concept of relaxed/poised living presented in this book.

Once relaxation and poise have been brought into the fabric of a life, they tend to alter attitudes, so that those which favour relaxed/poised living become prevalent. They include greater acceptance, tolerance, forgiveness, compassion, calmness, contemplation, un-hurriedness, openness, and so on. Maslow said that such attitudes went with the process of self-actualisation (the process of fulfilling human potential). Relaxation, we are justified in saying, contributes to the development of full humanness, and this is its profound-est aspect.

The art of creative relaxation is one that has to be learned on the basis of individual practice and experience. Personality and temperament will influence the form it takes, but the practical preparation is the same for all. The foundations for relaxed/poised living were described in the preceding chapters: daily dips into deep body–mind relaxation, meditation's mental hygiene, the practice of bare attention several times daily, making poised posture habitual, knowing what to do about coping with anger, fear, anxiety, and other destructive emotions, and adopting a life style that avoids unnecessary friction and stress, balancing activity and rest.

Working together, these practices produce the psychological equivalent of opening wide the windows of a house long allowed to be airless. The result is heightened awareness, more energy, and a broadening of attitudes and beliefs.

Life style

If your life style is causing you stress, think of practical ways by which you can streamline it and reduce friction. Look at the stress-rating scale given in Chapter 1; if you have high scores for recent months, be on guard against contributing unnecessarily to your current pressures. Some stresses come 'out of the blue' and you cannot prevent them; but at times when you have had enough excitement in recent months you will be in a position to avoid or postpone situations which are apt to send up your blood pressure and otherwise cause an arousal reaction.

There may be ways of cutting stress out of your life by making environmental changes. It may be helpful to change jobs, for example. However, radical changes in your life may be made unnecessary if you use relaxation techniques and take more 'philosophical' attitudes to things and events.

A wide perspective

An examination of attitudes and beliefs that are in accord with and support relaxed/poised living show most of them to be linked with taking a broad and philosophical (in the popular sense) view. This may be called a wide-angle view – it is rather like mentally switching camera lenses from a standard lens to a wide-angle lens that enables us to see more in the viewfinder. An alternative is to step back a few paces, a measure of detachment. The practice of meditation fosters detachment of a healthy kind. Normally we may be caught up in certain troublesome emotions, as though trapped in a quagmire; with meditative attention the quagmire is still there, but we view it from the edge, so to speak. Eventually our attitudes alter and events responsible for disturbing feelings are perceived differently, altering the feelings.

Telling yourself, when things are going badly, that 'there's always another day' or that 'time heals' is a commonplace example of adopting a relaxing attitude based on taking a broad view; in this illustration, a broad view of time. Dr Samuel Johnson told Boswell, who was 'uptight' over a personal problem: 'Come, sir, think how little you will think of this in ten years' time.'

Carried to its limit, this attitude can become a cosmic view in which things, happenings, and people are seen 'in the light of eternity'.

Experiencing 'the beautiful' relaxes. 'Beauty acts by relaxing the solids of the system', wrote Edmund Burke. Music, poetry, and the arts achieve their profoundest effects by broadening our vision, taking us up and out of our everyday selves.

Contemplation of great expanses of sea, earth, or sky releases stress and broadens our view of life. The effect may be therapeutic. Fears and anxieties tend to be blotted out or diminished to the size of the human figures in Chinese landscape paintings. Perspective has altered psychologically as well as visually. When the actress Lillah McCarthy was deserted by her husband, the playwright Harley Granville-Barker, she found a wise comforter in George Bernard Shaw. 'I found myself walking with dragging steps with Shaw beside me . . . up and down Adelphi Terrace. The weight upon me grew a little lighter and released the tears which would never come before . . . Presently I heard a voice in which all the gentleness and tenderness of the world was speaking. It said: "Look up, dear, look up to the heavens. There is more in life than this. There is much more."'

A shift to more 'philosophic' attitudes often comes to people in middle-age, but these attitudes may be cultivated at any age and tend to develop naturally in the person who practises relaxation skills and is fully aware of their value.

The important things to note about the wide perspective is that it introduces objective values and diminishes egotistical striving and straining. Things are seen in better proportion. The person who drops a chip from his or her shoulder after carrying it for months or years, usually does so because of a shift in attitude – by taking a broad view.

The strain of coping with noisy and very active children when we are tired will be eased if we can pause and stand back a little, recall that in general they are really a joy, see their life as a whole and as part of human continuity – 'earth hath childers everywhere', as James Joyce put it.

Not every reader will manage the tough-mindedness recommended by John Cowper Powys, who wrote in one of his manuals on the art of happiness that we can defuse our reactions to troublesome children or adults by picturing them as skeletons.

Another significant point to note is that the wide perspective promotes a steadying and slowing down of attention; time is taken to breathe easily and to really see and to otherwise experience.

Taking time

Changed attitudes towards the passing of time can eliminate one of the most dangerous forms of stress. The 'philosophic' person is aware that there is plenty of time and accepts its passing. An unhurried attitude protects body and mind against stress and enables us to take time to see more and to be more aware. If you are one of those people who are guilty of pressing body and mind too hard, fighting against the clock, then you need to train yourself to become aware of the problem and to remind yourself to slow down.

Research shows that the person always in a hurry and pressed for time is a prime candidate for coronary thrombosis. A few physicians in past centuries sensed the danger. Sir William Osler, an eminent Victorian physician, told his students: 'The ordinary high-pressure business or professional man suffering from angina may find relief, or even a cure, in the simple process of "slowing the engines".' Mark Twain, in characteristic style, complained that 'everybody is going faster but they ain't going no place.' Rush, hustle and bustle feature even more in American and European life today than they did in Mark Twain's lifetime.

Driving oneself too hard and being pressed for time are often tied up with other harmful attitudes – particularly unrealistic ambitions, perfectionism and a too serious competitiveness.

Change, complexity, competition – with new attitudes

Early in this book it was said that change, complexity and competition account for much of the stress characteristic of civilised life today. These particular sources of stress can be reduced through the attitudes we take to them. The relaxed person is equipped to welcome change for its diversity and fluidity, complexity for its fascination and challenge, and competition may either be enjoyed as an exhilarating game in which the winning is not everything or left to more headstrong types (rat races, after all, are for rats!).

We can be sure that, barring a nuclear holocaust, technological advance will proceed even faster than before, so that the problems of coping with change, complexity and competition will intensify.

Abraham Maslow wrote of the need to produce a new kind of human being who enjoys change and who is comfortable with it. Societies which can turn out the new 'Heraclitian' people will survive; those which cannot create such people will perish. This is probably too dramatic a presentation of what is, however, undoubtedly a real social problem.

At a personal level, what is required for growth and fulfilment is to welcome, and often delight in, life's flux and flow. Heraclitus said that we live in flux and that we cannot step in the same river twice.

The philosophical attitude that best accepts and enjoys the ceaseless flow of life may be described as Taoist. Maslow used this epithet repeatedly in describing the characteristics and values of the most psychologically healthy people. Philosophical Taoism, whose spirit continued in Zen rather than in the religion called Taoism, contains much of value for any person interested in acquiring relaxing attitudes. (I have elaborated on this topic in *Relaxation East and West*.) We can learn to accept and even to love change, for the diversity and fluidity it brings to living. How dull and oppressive life would be if all forms were forever fixed. We associate rigidity with death, fluidity with life. The Taoist Lao Tzu wrote in a Chinese classic, the *Tao Te Ching*:

'The greatest virtue is like water; it is good to all things.
It attains the most inaccessible places without strife.
Therefore it is like Tao.
It has the virtue of adapting itself to its place.
It is virtuous like the heart by being deep.
It is virtuous like speech by being faithful.
It is virtuous like government in regulating.
It is virtuous like a servant in its ability.
It is virtuous like action by being in season.
And because it does not strive it has no enemies.'
(tr. W. G. Old)

The Tao is the way or course of Nature.

Complexity denotes the evolutionary advance of humanity and should not prove overwhelming for a stable integrated organism. It can come to be enjoyed – just as many music-lovers progress from appreciating single melodies to finding interest and delight in more intricate works; the multi rhythms and tunes of Charles Ives, for example, with up to twenty separate musical strands simultaneously busy.

As for competitiveness, it can be enjoyed and be life-enhancing at a certain level – that of the 'good sportsman', for example – but becomes a danger to health at the level now habitual among a great many businessmen in the United States. Many Europeans seem hell bent on matching the Americans in this stressful attitude.

One way that many people can avoid unnecessary stress is to be realistic about their talents and prospects, though staying hopeful that they might do better than they think probable. Many people surprise themselves, and others, with their achievements, but many more have cherished unrealistic ambitions and been wounded painfully by failure to realise them. Much anxiety and resentment are caused by this failure; depression also.

Inferiority feelings are behind many cases of corrosive disappointment and frustration – yet it is only commonsense to see that we must expect to be behind some people in some respects and ahead of them in others. The person who has healthy relaxed attitudes can express his or her potential and accept each stage of life's journey for whatever interest and satisfaction it affords here and now, without feeling impelled to make excessive comparisons with others or constant reference to an exaggerated sense of self-worth.

You are certain to subject yourself to stress if you are victim of the habit of frequently comparing yourself to others in matters of occupational success, social status, material possessions, personal appearance, skills at games, and so on. It is a mistake to base self-worth on competitive performance standards. Many people will avoid considerable stress if they develop their own standards of self-worth and cease worrying about competition with others.

A perfectionist attitude often goes with the self-evaluating habit and causes tensions. Perfectionists often suffer from depression and frequently have nervous breakdowns.

The answer, then, for those of us cultivating relaxing attitudes is to be realistic about our abilities and to enjoy doing well by our own standards.

Such an attitude need not preclude our aiming for our own modicum of excellence in however humble an area – and perhaps in living itself. Excellence may be aimed for in running a country, a business empire or a small shop; in cultivating a small garden or a large farm; in sweeping a street, looking after children or repairing a motor-cycle (the last eloquently brought out by Robert M. Pirsig in his surprising best-seller *Zen and the Art of Motor Cycle Maintenance*).

Excellence – the ancient Greek virtue of *aretê* – is self-validating and only incidentally connected with winning and losing. It is deeply rewarding, emotionally, to do things that are worth doing in themselves.

Despite all that has been said about eliminating unnecessary muscle tension, anxiety, and stress, it would be unrealistic and probably not even desirable to anticipate a life of unbroken ease and tranquillity. Without challenges, problems to solve and obstacles to overcome, most people are soon bored. Normally life can be relied upon to provide them.

Some readers may agree with Dr Karl Menninger, an eminent American psychiatrist, when he says:

'Unrest of spirit is a mark of life; one problem after another presents itself and in the solving of them we can find our greatest pleasure. The continuous encounter with continually changing conditions is the very substance of living. From an acute awareness of the surging effort we have the periodic relief of seeing one task finished and another begun. . . . A querulous search for a premature permanent "peace" seems to me a thinly disguised wish to die.'

Temperament may have a bearing on how each of us registers the matter.

With positive attitudes to change, complexity, and competition, technological civilisation need not be unduly stressful. You can become more effective in life, and in a relaxed way.

References

Barker, Sarah, *The Alexander Technique: The Revolutionary Way to Use your Body for Total Energy*, Bantam Books, New York, 1978.

Benson, Herbert, *The Relaxation Response*, William Morrow, New York, 1976.

Byles, Marie Beuzeville, *Stand Straight Without Strain: the Original Exercises of F. Matthias Alexander*, Fowler, Romford, Essex, 1978.

Cannon, W. B., *The Wisdom of the Body*, Norton, New York, 1932.

Chesser, Eustace, *Life Is for Living (So Relax and Enjoy It)*, George G. Harrap, London, 1963.

Fenton, Jack Vinten, *The Choice of Habit*, Macdonald and Evans, London, 1973.

Frankl, Viktor E., *Psychotherapy and Existentialism*, Souvenir Press, London, 1970.

Friedman, Meyer and Rosenman, Ray H., *Type A Behaviour and Your Heart*, Knopf, New York, 1974.

Hewitt, James, *New Faces*, A. Thomas, Wellingborough, Northants, 1977.

Hewitt, James, *Meditation* (Teach Yourself Books), Hodder and Stoughton Educational, Dunton Green, Sevenoaks, Kent, 1978.

Hewitt, James, *Yoga* (Teach Yourself Books), Hodder and Stoughton Educational, Dunton Green, Sevenoaks, Kent, 1979.

Hewitt, James, *Isometrics: the Short Cut to Fitness*, Thorsons, Wellingborough, Northants, 1980.

Hewitt, James, *Relaxation East and West: A Manual of Poised Living*, Rider, London, 1982.

Hirai, Tomio, *Zen and the Mind: Scientific Approach to Zen Practice*, Tokyo, 1970.

Holmes, Thomas H. and Rahe, Richard H., 'The Social Readjustment Rating Scale', *Journal of Psychosomatic Research*, 11 (1967).

Horney, Karen, *New Ways in Psychoanalysis*, Routledge and Kegan Paul, London, 1939.

Jacobson, Edmund, *Progressive Relaxation*, University of Chicago Press, Chicago, 1929.

Jacobson, Edmund, *You Must Relax*, McGraw-Hill, New York, 1962.

Mackarness, Richard, *Not All in the Mind*, Pan Books, London, 1976.

Marks, Isaac H., *Living With Fear: Understanding and Coping*, McGraw-Hill, New York, 1978.

Maslow, Abraham H. and Mittelmann, Bela, *Principles of Abnormal Psychology*, Harper and Brothers, New York, revised edition 1951.

Maslow, Abraham H., *Toward a Psychology of Being*, D. Van Nostrand, New York, 1968.

Meares, Ainslie, *Relief Without Drugs: the Self-management of Tension, Anxiety, and Pain*, Doubleday, New York, 1967.

Meichenbaum, Donald H., *Cognitive Behaviour Modification*, Plenum, New York, 1977.

Menninger, Karl, in Bernard H. Hall, ed., *A Psychiatrist's World*, Viking, New York, 1959.

Morris, Desmond, *The Human Zoo*, Jonathan Cape, London, 1980.

Neuhaus, Heinrich, *The Art of Piano Playing*, Barrie and Jenkins, London, 1973.

Parsonage, Maurice, in John H. C. Colson, ed., *Postural and Relaxation Training in Physiotherapy and Physical Education*, Heinemann, London, second edition, 1968.

Pirsig, Robert M., *Zen and the Art of Motorcycle Maintenance*, The Bodley Head, 1974.

Powys, John Cowper, *In Defence of Sensuality*, Victor Gollancz, London, 1930; Village Press, London, 1974.

Rosa, Karl Robert, *Autogenic Training,* Victor Gollancz, London, 1976.

Rushdall, Brent S., *Psyching in Sport*, Pelham Books, London, 1979.

Schultz, Johannes H. and Luthe, W., *Autogenic Therapy*, vols 1–5, Grune and Stratton, New York, 1969.

Selye, Hans, *The Stress of Life*, McGraw-Hill, New York, 1956.

Sillitoe, Alan, *Her Victory*, W. H. Allen, 1982.

Wallace, R. K. and Benson, H., 'The Physiology of Meditation', *Scientific American* **226** (1972).

Weekes, Claire, *Self-help for Your Nerves*, Angus and Robertson, London, 1962.

Whitehill, James, *Enter the Quiet: Everyone's Way to Meditation*, Harper and Row, New York, 1980.

Whone, Herbert, *The Simplicity of Playing the Violin*, Victor Gollancz, 1972.

Index